Airline Liveries

Fourth Edition

Günter Endres

G-BOAF

Ian Allan
PUBLISHING

INTRODUCTION

The airline industry has entered into its most colourful period to date, highlighted by the growing number of British Airways 'World Images' created by artists from around the world. Although these have received a mixed reception, British Airways is continuing with the process, eventually planning to have 50 different schemes adorning its aircraft. While this has been tried on a smaller scale before — Alaska Airlines and Frontier Airlines in the US are prime examples — this is the first attempt by a leading intercontinental carrier to break away from tradition. Many airlines are also making use of anniversaries and other occasions to paint one or two aircraft in special schemes, and there is an increasing trend by airlines to maximise revenues by allowing aircraft to be painted as flying advertising boards.

For the purists, this is perhaps the most unwelcome trend, but for the enthusiast, it provides seemingly endless opportunities for discovery, to which can be added the many hybrid schemes that appear at the world's airports as the incidence of temporary leases mushrooms. The changing and modernisation of the corporate image as a 'total concept' is a continuing process. It serves to facilitate instant recognition and aims to create a unique identity that sets one company apart from another. In today's highly competitive environment, image and service, both inside the aircraft and out, are among the prime tools available to airlines to make it into the next millennium.

Günter Endres
Lindfield

ACKNOWLEDGEMENTS

It always comes as a surprise to realise the considerable changes that occur in the two years between editions. More than 10 airlines have introduced new corporate images, not to mention changes to route structures and fleets. The book has also been expanded by another 20 airlines, giving yet more insight into the development of colour schemes. Without the direct help of many of the airlines featured, the task of bringing the coverage right up to date would have been far more difficult. My sincere appreciation also goes to Alan J. Wright and Terry Shone, as well as David Velupillai of Airbus Industrie, Colin Fisher of Bombardier Regional Aircraft and Julie Green of the Boeing News Bureau in London, for supplying the majority of the photographs.

Front cover: Virgin and British Airways tails. *Austin J. Brown/Aviation Picture Library*

Back cover: A colourful selection of tails. *Richard Cooper*

Previous page: Various liveries can be seen in this view. *Author*

Picture Credits:
All photographs are via the author and come from manufacturers' and airlines' files unless otherwise credited.

First published 1999

ISBN 0 7110 2650 5

© Ian Allan Publishing Ltd 1999

Published by Ian Allan Publishing

an imprint of Ian Allan Publishing Ltd, Terminal House, Shepperton, Surrey TW17 8AS.
Printed by Ian Allan Printing Ltd, Riverdene Business Park, Hersham, Surrey KT12 4RG.

Code: 9905/E

CONTENTS

AB AIRLINES (7L/AZX)

Founded/First Service: 8 February 1993/11 October 1993 as Air Bristol
Bases: London Gatwick and London Stansted airports, United Kingdom
Services: Low-fare airline providing scheduled passenger services from London Gatwick to Shannon in Ireland, and to Barcelona, Berlin Schönefeld, Lisbon and Nice (operated in a codeshare arrangement with Debonair), and to Palma de Mallorca (with Futura International). Another schedule links Shannon to Birmingham and London Stansted, flown as a codeshare with Irish flag-carrier Aer Lingus. A North Atlantic partnership is being planned.
Fleet: 3 x Boeing 737-300, 3 x British Aerospace (BAC) 111-500.
On order: 6 x Boeing 737-700.
Colour Scheme: The initials 'AB' are displayed prominently in two shades of green — mid-green and jade — on the maroon tail fin, which elegantly wraps around the rear of the white fuselage, following the line of the leading-edge. The same arrangement is repeated on the engine cowlings. 'AB AIRLINES' titles sit above the front set of windows, also in maroon, ahead of a 'FIRST FOR VALUE' inscription in green. The whole is underlined by a thin green pencil line speeding along the fuselage and widening at the rear into the maroon band.
Illustrated: Boeing 737-300

ADRIA AIRWAYS (JP/ADR)

Founded/First Service: 1961
Base: Brnik Airport, Ljubljana, Slovenia
Services: National airline of Slovenia, providing international scheduled services from Ljubljana to Amsterdam, Barcelona, Brussels, Copenhagen, Frankfurt, London Heathrow, Manchester (summer only), Moscow, Munich, Ohrid, Paris, Sarajevo, Skopje, Split, Tel Aviv, Tirana, Vienna and Zürich. Charter flights are operated to destinations in Europe and North Africa, particularly to Antalya and Istanbul in Turkey, Tunis, Athens and Las Palmas de Gran Canaria in the Canary Islands.
Fleet: 3 x Airbus A320-200, 3 x Bombardier (Canadair) CRJ-200LR
Colour Scheme: Large and bold 'Adria' titles in blue take up half of the clean all-white fuselage, being highly visible from a distance. The airline's insignia, which depicts the first letter 'A' in blue reflected in the turquoise waters of the Adriatic, dominates the tail fin. On the Airbus A320, the insignia is repeated on the engine cowlings.
Illustrated: Bombardier CRJ-200LR.

AER LINGUS (EI/EIN)

Founded/First Service: 22 May 1936
Base: Dublin Airport, Dublin, Irish Republic
Services: Irish flag-carrier with a concentration of European routes and long-haul flights to Boston, Chicago, Newark and New York JFK. A Los Angeles service will be added in summer 1999. European and UK destinations are Amsterdam, Belfast, Birmingham, Bristol, Brussels, Copenhagen, Düsseldorf, Edinburgh, Frankfurt, Glasgow, Jersey, Leeds/Bradford, London Heathrow, London Stansted, Madrid, Manchester, Milan, Newcastle, Paris, Rennes, Rome and Zürich. A domestic route system includes Cork, Dublin, Galway, Kerry County, Shannon and Sligo, and these together with some UK provincial cities are served under the name of Aer Lingus Commuter. Spanish-based associate Futura provides mainly holiday charter flights, in addition to a Palma de Mallorca-London Gatwick schedule.
Subsidiaries and Associates: Futura International Airlines (85%)
Fleet: 2 x Airbus A321-200, 5 x A330-300, 6 x Boeing 737-400, 9 x 737-500.
On order: 6 x Airbus A320-200, 4 x A321-200
Aer Lingus Commuter: 2 x British Aerospace 146-200, 5 x 146-300, 6 x Fokker 50
Colour Scheme: The Aer Lingus corporate identity was launched on 14 February 1996 with a concept developed by Luxon Carra, designed to capture the essence of the airline: Irish, vibrant, dynamic, responsive, natural and 'green'. It features a reworked shamrock with more fluid and natural lines on the tail fin and softer colours of three shades of green, a petrol blue and a grey, covering the upper part of the crisp white fuselage. This is said to evoke a lush and verdant landscape, interspersed with clean lakes and rivers and overcast with mist-laden skies. The name is applied forward in a flowing typography, resembling the written word and reminiscent of a new literary theme embodied in excerpts from the writings of Irish poets, novelists and playwrights, reproduced on many airline items.
Illustrated: Airbus A330-300

AEROFLOT RUSSIAN INTERNATIONAL AIRLINES (SU/AFL)

Founded/First Service: 9 February 1923 as Dobrolet; Aeroflot name adopted in 1932 but reorganised under the present title in July 1992

Base: Moscow Sheremetievo Airport, Moscow, Russia

Services: Russia's principal international airline, flying to 147 destinations in 77 countries and providing two-thirds of all international routes served by the country's airlines. Airbridges in the former Soviet Union connect Moscow with around 40 cities in Russia, the Commonwealth of Independent States (CIS) and the Baltic states. European cities on the network include Amsterdam, Ankara, Athens, Belgrade, Berlin, Bourgas, Bratislava, Brussels, Budapest, Bucharest, Copenhagen, Dresden, Dublin, Dubrovnik, Düsseldorf, Erfurt, Frankfurt, Gdansk, Geneva, Hamburg, Helsinki, Istanbul, Leipzig, Lisbon, London, Luxembourg, Madrid, Malta, Marseille, Milan, Munich, Nicosia, Oslo, Paris, Prague, Rome, Salzburg, Sofia, Shannon, Stockholm, Tampere, Vienna, Warsaw, Zagreb and Zürich.

Fleet: 10 x A310-300, 6 x Boeing 737-400, 2 x 767-300ER, 2 x 777-200ER, 22 x Ilyushin IL-62M, 13 x IL-76TD, 20 x IL-86, 6 x IL-96-300, 1 x McDonnell Douglas DC-10-30CF, 12 x Tupolev Tu-134A, 29 Tu-154M.

On order: 4 x Boeing 737-400, 17 x Ilyushin IL-96M, 3 x IL-96T

Colour Scheme: A new Aeroflot corporate identity was introduced during 1998. It makes imaginative use of the national colours of red, white and blue, with the tail fin treated as a canvas with broad brush strokes in all three colours. The oil-painting effect is repeated on the engine cowlings. The rest of the aircraft remains rather conventional with a broad window line in blue, underscored by a thin pencil line. Traditional 'Aeroflot' titles in Cyrillic lettering, together with its long-established winged hammer and sickle motif, are applied in blue on the upper fuselage, forward of the wing and alongside the Russian flag. So far only the Boeing 737-400 is painted in this scheme, with the rest of the fleet still featuring the Russian flag on an all-white tail fin.

Illustrated: Boeing 737-400

AEROLINEAS ARGENTINAS (AR/ARG)

Founded/First Service: May 1949
Bases: Ministro Pistarini International and Aeroparque Jorge Newbery airports, Buenos Aires, Argentina
Services: National airline operating scheduled passenger and cargo services throughout the Americas, and across the Atlantic to Amsterdam, Frankfurt, London Heathrow, Madrid, Paris, Rome and Zürich, and to Sydney and Auckland across the Pacific. The network in the Americas links Buenos Aires to Asunçion, Bogotá, Caracas, Havana, La Paz, Mexico City, Miami, Montevideo, New York, Punta del Este, Rio de Janeiro, Santa Cruz de la Sierra, Santiago de Chile and São Paulo. Main domestic routes are those between the capital and Comodoro Rivadavia, Cordoba, Mar del Plata and Rosario, backed up by further extensive services to over 30 towns and cities by subsidiary Austral.
Subsidiaries and Associates: Austral Lineas Aéreas (100%)
Fleet: 2 x Airbus A310-300, 5 x Boeing 737-200, 1 x 737-200C, 13 x 737-200 Advanced, 9 x 747-200B, 1 x Boeing (McDonnell Douglas) MD-83, 6 x MD-88.
On order: 4 x Airbus A320-200, 2 x A340-300, 6 x A340-600
Austral: 2 x CASA CN-235-200, 2 x Boeing (McDonnell Douglas) MD-81, 2 x MD-83, 2 x McDonnell Douglas DC-9-31, 2 x DC-9-32
Colour Scheme: Aerolineas Argentinas' present livery features twin cheatlines in light and royal blue on an otherwise all-white aircraft, which sweep down from behind the cockpit and along the fuselage at and above window level. The traditional condor insignia in royal blue is the only splash of colour on the tail fin. 'AEROLINEAS ARGENTINAS' titles are reversed out in white and set into the upper royal blue cheatline at mid-fuselage.
Illustrated: Boeing 747-200B

AERO LLOYD (YP/AEF)

Founded/First Service: 5 December 1980/1 April 1981
Base: Frankfurt Rhein/Main Airport, Frankfurt, Germany
Services: Prominent German charter airline operating inclusive-tour charters from Berlin, Düsseldorf, Frankfurt and Hamburg to resorts in the Mediterranean basin and the Canary Islands. Typical destinations include Adana, Alicante, Almeria, Amman, Antalya, Arrecife, Catania, Chania, Corfu, Faro, Fuerteventura, Heraklion, Hurghada, Ibiza, Kefalonia, Kos, Las Palmas de Gran Canaria, Lisbon, Luxor, Mahon, Malaga, Marrakech, Monastir, Mykonos, Naples, Olbia, Palma de Mallorca, Rhodes, Santorini, Sharm-el-Sheikh, Tel Aviv, Thessaloniki and Zakynthos.
Fleet: 6 x Airbus A320-200, 3 x A321-200, 10 x Boeing (McDonnell Douglas) MD-83
On order: 7 x Airbus A321-200
Colour Scheme: Aero Lloyd's present simpler but effective scheme was introduced with the delivery of the Airbus A320s in early 1996. The clean white fuselage is adorned only with the company's blue and red symbol, a clever transformation of the letters 'L' and 'A' into a speed arrow on the tail fin, repeated on the engine cowlings. The same colour combination is used in the airline's name in capital letters, ahead of the wing and below the cabin windows. The blue and red colours also appear on the winglets of the Airbuses.
Illustrated: Airbus A320-200

AEROMEXICO (AM/AMX)

Founded/First Service: 15 September 1934 as Aeronaves de Mexico, present name adopted 28 January 1972

Base: Benito Juarez International Airport, Mexico City, Mexico

Services: Mexico's major airline serving a vast domestic network of 40 towns and cities, together with scheduled cross-border services to the United States and across the Atlantic to Madrid and Paris in Europe. US destinations are Atlanta, Dallas/Fort Worth, Houston, Miami, Los Angeles, New Orleans, New York JFK, Orlando, Phoenix, Salt Lake City, San Diego and Tucson, and there is also a Mexico City-São Paulo connection. Marketing, codeshare and block-space agreement with other airlines further extends its international system. The domestic network is supported with feeder services by Aeroliteral, while Aeromexpress operates all-freighter flights.

Subsidiaries and Associates: Aeroliteral (100%), Aeromexpress (100%), AeroPeru (35%)

Fleet: 6 x Boeing 757-200, 2 x 767-200ER, 2 x 767-300ER, 11 x Boeing (McDonnell Douglas) MD-82, 7 x MD-83, 2 x MD-87, 10 x MD-88, 2 x McDonnell Douglas DC-9-31, 15 x DC-9-32

Colour Scheme: The present livery was introduced following the airline's privatisation in 1988. Its central feature is the famous Mexican birdman motif on a mid-blue tail fin, with the airline name at the base, given a speed emphasis through a blue and white gradation of the word 'Aero'. The blue extends the length of the fuselage in a broad window stripe, underscored by a lower red cheatline of the same width, the two lines separating the roof from the lower fuselage, both finished in natural metal. The colours reflect the national flag, which is carried above the front cabin windows.

Illustrated: Boeing 757-200. *Terry Shone*

AIR 2000 (DP/AMM)

Founded/First Service: 11 April 1987
Bases: Manchester Airport, Manchester, and London Gatwick, United Kingdom
Services: Major holiday charter airline with intensive charter programmes from Manchester, London Gatwick, Birmingham, Bristol, Glasgow, Newcastle and smaller provincial airports to the principal holiday destinations around the Mediterranean, together with long-haul flights to South Africa, the United States and the Caribbean. Scheduled leisure routes are also operated to Larnaca and Paphos in Cyprus from Birmingham, London Gatwick and Manchester. A specially-configured Boeing 757 in a luxury 92-seat layout is used on specialist charters, such as 'Around the World', 'Around Africa' and 'Around South America' tours. During the winter season, aircraft are leased out to Canadian Royal Aviation.
Fleet: 6 x Airbus A320-200, 3 x A321-200, 13 x Boeing 757-200, 2 x 767-300.
On order: 2 x Airbus A321-200, 2 x A330-200, 2 x Boeing 767-300ER
Colour Scheme: The airline's look combines the distinctive colours of its parent company First Choice with evocative holiday images from around the world through a tapestry of vivid colours and bold shapes. The distinctive 'swoop' shape of the tapestry on the sides was inspired by the aircraft's aerodynamic qualities and adds to its visual momentum, while the unique use of the tapestry's colours on both upper and lower wings takes advantage of a previously little-exploited device for communicating identity. 'Air 2000' titles are applied in blue above the forward cabin windows.
Illustrated: Boeing 757-200

Air 2000

AIR AFRIQUE (RK/RKA)

Founded/First Service: 28 March 1961/15 October 1961 as multinational carrier for 11 former French colonies
Base: Félix Houphouet-Boigny International Airport, Abidjan, Ivory Coast
Services: Multinational flag-carrier of Benin, Burkina Faso, Central African Republic, Chad, Congo, Guinea, Ivory Coast, Mali, Mauritania, Niger, Senegal and Togo. Scheduled passenger and cargo services are flown throughout Central and West Africa, connecting the capital cities of the member states, and to Europe, the Middle East and the United States. Cities served are Abu Dhabi, Accra, Bamako, Bangui, Banjul, Bissau, Brazzaville, Bordeaux, Conakry, Cotonou, Dakar, Douala, Freetown, Geneva, Jeddah, Johannesburg, Lagos, Libreville, Lisbon, Lomé, Lyon, Malabo, Marseille, New York JFK, N'Djamena, Niamey, Nouakchott, Ouagadougou, Paris CDG, Pointe Noire and Rome. Also from Abidjan to New York via Dakar, Senegal.
Subsidiaries and Associates: Air Mali (46%), Air Mauritanie (20%), Air Burkina (17%)
Fleet: 3 x Airbus A300B4-200, 2 x A300-600R, 4 x A310-300, 1 x Antonov An-12, 1 x Boeing 737-200C Advanced, 2 x 737-300, 1 x 707-320C, 1 x McDonnell Douglas DC-10-30
Colour Scheme: As a multinational carrier, Air Afrique chose neutral bright shades of lime green and emerald green to colour the broad cheatlines, with the lime green along the windows and the emerald below. The aircraft is otherwise snow-white. Centrepiece of the tail is a gazelle's head spanning a globe, both in matching emerald green, symbolising the airline's far-reaching and speedy service. Bold 'Air Afrique' titles in a classic black typeface are displayed on the forward upper fuselage.
Illustrated: Airbus A310-300

AIR ALGÉRIE (AH/DAH)

Founded/First Service: 1946 as Compagnie Générale de Transports Aériens (CGTA), present name adopted in April 1953 after merger with Compagnie Air Transport (CAT)
Base: Houari Boumedienne Airport, Algiers, Algeria
Services: National flag-carrier operating scheduled passenger and cargo services to destinations in North and West Africa, Europe and the Middle East. International destinations served include Amman, Bamako, Barcelona, Berlin, Brussels, Cairo, Casablanca, Dakar, Damascus, Frankfurt, Geneva, Istanbul, Lille, London Heathrow, Lyon, Madrid, Marseille, Moscow, Niamey, Nice, Nouakchott, Ouagadougou, Palma de Mallorca, Paris CDG, Prague, Rome, Sharjah, Toulouse, Tunis and Warsaw. An extensive domestic network is also operated, together with air taxi and agricultural flying.
Fleet: 1 x Aérospatiale SE3130 Alouette II, 4 x Airbus A310-200,
3 x Beechcraft 65-B80 Queen Air, 2 x King Air A100, 7 x Bell 206L-3 LongRanger III,
2 x Boeing 727-200, 9 x 727-200 Advanced, 13 x 737-200 Advanced, 2 x 737-200C Advanced,
3 x 767-300, 7 x Fokker F27-400M, 2 x Lockheed L-100-30 Hercules, 1 x L-1329 JetStar II
On order: 3 x Boeing 737-600, 7 x 737-800
Colour Scheme: Introduced in mid-1982, the paint scheme is built around the national colours of red, green and white and features two thin red stripes separated by a broader green band. The upper red cheatline sweeps up and over the rear fuselage into a wide sash. An all-white tail displays the company's red insignia, said to represent its two-letter code 'AH' in the shape of a bird. English and Arabic titles are applied side-by-side on the upper fuselage.
Illustrated: Boeing 727-200

13

AIR BALTIC (BT/BTI)

Founded/First Service: 23 July 1992 as Baltic International Airlines (BIA), present title adopted 1 October 1995 when merged with Latavio

Base: Riga International Airport, Riga, Latvia

Services: National flag-carrier providing international scheduled passenger and cargo services from Riga to Copenhagen, Frankfurt, Hamburg, Helsinki, Kiev, Minsk, Moscow, London Heathrow, Stockholm, Tallinn, Vilnius and Warsaw. The Copenhagen and Stockholm services are operated in a codeshare arrangement with Scandinavian Airlines System (SAS) and the Frankfurt route in a codeshare with Lufthansa. Partially privatised in 1995, with SAS holding a 28.5% stake, since increased to 34%.

Fleet: 3 x British Aerospace (Avro) RJ70, 2 x Saab 340A

Colour Scheme: The colour scheme has been evolving since the airline started operations following independence. The present identity, first adopted on the Saab 340A, has a clean look, distinguished by an all-white fuselage and a blue and white checkerboard tail fin. 'airBaltic' titles in blue, with the letter 'B' tilted and designed to match the tail application, are painted low on the forward fuselage. The airline title is repeated on the white engine cowlings. The national flag of maroon and white appears alongside the rear door of the aircraft.

Illustrated: Avro RJ70. *Terry Shone*

AIR CANADA (AC/ACA)

Founded/First Service: 10 April 1937 as Trans-Canada Airlines/1 September 1937, present title adopted 1 January 1965

Base: Dorval Airport, Montreal, Quebec, Canada

Services: Canada's largest airline, providing passenger and cargo services to the United States and the Caribbean, together with trans-Pacific routes to Seoul, Hong Kong and Osaka, and across the North Atlantic to Europe, Tel Aviv and Delhi. Destinations in Europe include Frankfurt, Glasgow, London Heathrow, Manchester, Paris and Zürich. All major domestic points are scheduled, with feeder services provided by four regional airlines under the *Air Canada Connector* network. Air Canada is a member of the *Star Alliance*, which also includes Lufthansa, SAS, Thai Airways International, United Airlines and Varig Brazilian Airlines, which together offer a far-reaching network with over 600 destinations in 108 countries.

Subsidiaries and Associates: Air Alliance (100%), AirBC (100%), Air Ontario (100%) and Air Nova (100%)

Fleet: 35 x Airbus A319, 34 x A320-200, 9 x A340-300, 3 x Boeing 747-100, 3 x 747-200B Combi, 3 x 747-400 Combi, 10 x 767-200, 13 x 767-200ER, 6 x 767-300ER, 25 x Bombardier (Canadair) CRJ-100ER, 25 x McDonnell Douglas DC-9-32

On order: 5 x Airbus A330-200, 3 x A340-300, 2 x A340-500, 3 x A340-300

Colour Scheme: Prominent red 'AIR CANADA' titles on a simple white body are preceded by the familiar, yet more natural looking roundel. A huge red maple leaf against an evergreen background on the tail symbolises the land, its people, its strength and its airline. The green is also reproduced on the winglets of the Airbuses, 747-400s and the Canadair Regional Jet. Unveiled on 1 December 1993, the new identity was created by New York-based consultants, Dieffenbach Elkins to reflect Air Canada's evolution from a Crown corporation to a fully-privatised carrier, while retaining its attributes of tradition, stability and reliability.

Illustrated: Bombardier (Canadair) CRJ-100ER

AIR CANADA

AIR CHINA (CA/CCA)

Founded/First Service: 2 November 1949 as part of the Civil Aviation Administration of China (CAAC), adopted present title in July 1988
Base: Beijing Capital Airport, Beijing, People's Republic of China
Services: China's largest airline serving mostly regional and intercontinental services from Beijing to Addis Ababa, Bangkok, Copenhagen, Frankfurt, Fukuoka, Helsinki, Kuwait, London, Melbourne, Milan, Moscow, New York, Osaka, Paris, Rome, San Francisco, Sendai, Seoul, Singapore, Stockholm, Sydney, Tokyo, Ulan Bator, Vancouver, Vienna, Yangon and Zürich. Regional flights to Rangoon, Bangkok, Singapore, Manila, Pyongyang, Osaka, Nagasaki, Fukuoka and Tokyo. Apart from Beijing, other cities linked into the international network are Dalian, Guangzhou, Kunming, Shanghai and Xiamen. An extensive domestic trunk network is also operated.
Fleet: 3 x Airbus A340-300, 19 x Boeing 737-300, 5 x 747-400, 6 x 747-400 Combi, 1 x 747-200B Combi, 2 x 747-200F, 4 x 747SP, 6 x 767-200ER, 4 x 767-300, 2 x 777-200, 4 x British Aerospace 146-100, 2 x Lockheed L-100-30 Hercules, 2 x Xi'an Y7-100C
Colour Scheme: A white upper fuselage and grey underside are separated by twin mid-blue cheatlines of different width, the lower covering the window level. Black 'AIR CHINA' titles in English and Chinese characters are preceded by the red national flag incorporating the five-pointed yellow stars. A stylised red phoenix, said by the Chinese to bring good fortune, flies on the white tail. On the Airbus A340 and Boeing 747-400, the phoenix is repeated on the winglets.
Illustrated: Boeing 747-400

AIR EUROPA (UX/AEA)

Founded/First Service: 17 February 1984/November 1986
Base: Palma de Mallorca Airport, Palma de Mallorca, Balearic Islands, Spain
Services: Spanish independent airline specialising in inclusive-tour services between northern Europe and the Balearic and Canary Islands, but increasingly moving into scheduled passenger services. European schedules include Belfast, Cardiff, London Gatwick, Oslo and Paris Charles de Gaulle, but Air Europa also flies across the Atlantic to Havana in Cuba and to New York J. F. Kennedy. Its domestic network encompasses all major Spanish cities and holiday resorts, including Alicante, Arrecife, Barcelona, Bilbao, Fuerteventura, Las Palmas de Gran Canaria, Ibiza, Madrid, Mahon, Malaga, Oviedo, Palma de Mallorca, Salamanca, Santiago, Seville, Tenerife North, Tenerife South, Valencia, Valladolid and Zaragoza. Some of these cities are served in a franchise arrangement with national carrier Iberia, signed in January 1998, and with subsidiary, Air Europa Express, concentrating on flights within the Canary Islands.
Subsidiaries and Associates: Air Europa Express (100%)
Fleet: 12 x Boeing 737-300, 6 x 737-400, 6 x 757-200, 4 x 767-300ER.
On order: 10 x Boeing 737-800
Air Europa Express: 5 x British Aerospace ATP
Colour Scheme: An appropriate sunshine image has been created by the warm red, orange and yellow cheatlines, contrasting with the pure white fuselage and engine finish. The cheatlines flow from similarly coloured 'AE' initials along the fuselage, terminating in a 'fanning' sweep up the tail fin. 'Air Europa' titles appear in black, lower case lettering on the tail, and on the forward upper fuselage accompanied by the Spanish flag.
Illustrated: Boeing 737-400. *Terry Shone*

air europa

AIR FRANCE (AF/AFR)

Founded/First Service: 30 August 1933

Bases: Paris Charles de Gaulle Airport, Roissy, and Paris Orly, France

Services: Scheduled passenger and cargo services worldwide, linking France with 233 towns and cities on all continents. Extensive route network within Europe serves 66 destinations, plus another 33 in metropolitan France, backed up by a number of franchise operations with regional airlines in France and the United Kingdom. Night mail services are flown for Administration Postale.

Subsidiaries and Associates: Franchises: Brit Air, City Jet, Gill Airways, Jersey European Airways, Proteus Airlines and Regional Airlines.

Fleet: 5 x Aérospatiale/BAe Concorde 100, 7 x Airbus A310-200, 3 x A310-300, 9 x A319, 7 x A320-100, 54 x A320-200, 11 x A321, 3 x A340-200, 11 x A340-300, 19 x Boeing 737-200 Advanced, 6 x 737-300, 18 x 737-500, 5 x 747-100, 12 x 747-200B, 12 x 747-200F, 2 x 747-300(SCD), 6 x 747-400, 6 x 747-400(SCD), 5 x 767-300ER, 4 x 777-200ER, 5 x Fokker 100.

On order: 6 x A319, 6 x Boeing 777-200ER

Colour Scheme: Based on the French Tricolour, the pure white overall fuselage finish is highlighted by bold blue 'AIR FRANCE' titles in upper case lettering, led by its long-established winged seahorse symbol in blue and red. The aircraft's major design element is a splash of colour in the form of blue and red stripes in varying widths sweeping up the tail fin. The colour scheme was introduced in 1975.

Illustrated: Boeing 777-200

AIR GABON (GN/AGN)

Founded/First Service: 1 June 1977
Base: Léon M'Ba International Airport, Libreville, Gabon
Services: International flag services to London, Marseille, Nice, Paris, Rome and Dubai, and regionally to Abidjan, Bamako, Bangui, Bata, Conakry, Cotonou, Dakar, Douala, Johannesburg, Kinshasa, Lomé, Lagos, Luanda, Malabo, Nairobi, Pointe Noire and São Tomé e Principe. The domestic network links the main towns of Franceville, Koulamoutou, Lastourville, Makokou, Mouila, Oyem, Port Gentil and Tchibanga, and the smaller communities of Gamba, Mayumba, Mitzic, Moanda and Ndende.
Fleet: 1 x Boeing 747-200B Combi, 1 x 767-200ER, 1 x 727-200 Advanced, 2 x 737-200C, 1 x Fokker F28-2000, 1 x Antonov An-12 (cargo)
Colour Scheme: The pure white finish of the aircraft fuselage is further freshened by the airline's stylised green parrot symbol on the tail fin, and 'AIR GABON' titles in blue on the forward cabin roof. A patriotic tricolour cheatline in the green, yellow and red colours of the national flag runs below the windows and extends the length of the fuselage, cut off at an angle at both ends. The colour green stands for the Gabonese forests, yellow for the warm sun, and blue for the abundant sea.
Illustrated: Boeing 747-200ER. *Terry Shone*

AIR-INDIA (AI/AIC)

Founded/First Service: 8 March 1948/8 June 1948
Base: Mumbai (Bombay) Airport, Mumbai, India
Services: Provides international flag services from Mumbai, Ahmedabad, Bangalore, Calcutta, Chennai (Madras), Delhi, Goa, Hyderabad and Thiruvananthapuram (Trivandrum) to destinations in the Asia Pacific, Middle East and Gulf, Africa, Europe and North America. Cities served are Abu Dhabi, Bahrain, Bangkok, Chicago, Dar-es-Salaam, Dhahran, Doha, Dubai, Frankfurt, Hong Kong, Jakarta, Jeddah, Kuala Lumpur, Kuwait, London Heathrow, Manchester, Moscow, Muscat, Nairobi, New York, Osaka, Paris, Riyadh, Rome, Singapore, Tokyo and Toronto. The airline has major code-share and block-seat agreements with Air Mauritius, Kuwait Airways, SAS, Singapore Airlines, Swissair and United Airlines, which extend its reach to many other cities. Air-India also operates services from Kozhikode to the Gulf, and hub and spoke operations out of Mumbai and Delhi to Hyderabad and Ahmedabad, jointly with Indian Airlines.
Fleet: 3 x Airbus A300B4-200, 8 x A310-300, 7 x Boeing 747-200B, 2 x Boeing 747-300 Combi, 6 x 747-400
Colour Scheme: Air-India's distinctive colour scheme sets it apart from other airlines. The windows are fashioned into graceful Rajasthani-style arches in red, which produce the effect of a row of Jharoka-type balconies reminiscent of the Hawa Mahal balconies of Jaipur. The whole design is framed in red. The aircraft are painted in white above and silver below the window line, with the titles, also in red, painted both in Hindi and English, and preceded by the national flag. 'AIR-INDIA' titles also sit atop a red fin flash.
Illustrated: Airbus A310-300

AIR JAMAICA (JM/AJM)

Founded/First Service: 1968/1 April 1969
Base: Norman Manley International Airport, Kingston, Jamaica
Services: Privatised national airline providing regional and international passenger services
from Kingston and Montego Bay to Atlanta, Baltimore/Washington, Chicago, Fort
Lauderdale, Los Angeles, Miami, New York/JFK and Newark, Orlando and Philadelphia in the
US, Antigua, Barbados, Grand Cayman, Havana, Providenciales and St Lucia in the Caribbean
and Central America, and across the Atlantic to London Heathrow. Inter-island services
linking Kingston, Montego Bay, Negril and Port Antonio, are operated by Air Jamaica Express,
previously known as Trans-Jamaican Airlines.
Subsidiaries and Associates: Air Jamaica Express (55%)
Fleet: 4 x Airbus A320-200, 6 x A310-300, 2 x Boeing 727-200 Advanced,
2 x Boeing (McDonnell Douglas) MD-83
Air Jamaica Express: 1 x Britten-Norman BN-2B Islander, 2 x Dornier 228-200,
2 x Shorts 360-300
Colour Scheme: The 'Jamaican Flair' colours were introduced following the airline's
privatisation in November 1984, intended to give a clear message that it is a new,
professional company facing the future with confidence. The splash of bright Caribbean
colours, taking over most of the aircraft surface, graduate in varying size bands from golden
yellow to orange, magenta and deep purple, ending in a sweep at the rear. The deep purple
covers the tail fin and is itself interspersed with magenta and lighter blue stripes. Dominating
the tail is Air Jamaica's traditional symbol of a yellow doctor bird, a native of Jamaica. 'air
Jamaica' titles in magenta and purple sit atop the orange band on the forward cabin roof.
Illustrated: Airbus A320-200

AIRLANKA (UL/ALK)

Founded/First Service: 10 January 1979/1 September 1979
Base: Bandaranayake International Airport, Colombo, Sri Lanka
Services: Sri Lankan flag-carrier operating international scheduled passenger and cargo services from Colombo to destinations in Asia, the Middle East and Europe. Cities served include Abu Dhabi, Amsterdam, Bahrain, Bangkok, Chennai (Madras), Dhahran, Delhi, Doha, Dubai, Frankfurt, Fukuoka, Hong Kong, Jeddah, Karachi, Kuala Lumpur, Kuwait, London Heathrow, Malé, Mumbai (Bombay), Muscat, Paris, Riyadh, Rome, Singapore, Tiruchirapalli, Thiruvananthapuram (Trivandrum), Tokyo and Zürich. Emirates Airline acquired a 26% stake and management control of the airline on 1 April 1998.
Fleet: 2 x Airbus A320-200, 3 x A340-300, 1 x Lockheed L-1011-100 TriStar, 1 x L-1011-50 TriStar, 2 x L-1011-500 TriStar.
On order: 6 x Airbus A330-200
Colour Scheme: A bright red windowline runs from the nose and spreads out over the entire rear fuselage and tail fin, which forms the backdrop to a large white stylised peacock motif. A thinner red cheatline accompanies the windowline along the whole length of the aircraft. The fuselage is finished in white, with black 'AIRLANKA' titles in capital letters forward of the wing. The Sri Lankan national flag, based on the Sinhalese flag and incorporating a golden lion with sword, framed by four Buddhist pipul leaves, and green and orange stripes to represent Hindu and Muslim minorities, is applied ahead of the airline name.
Illustrated: Airbus A320-200

AIR LITTORAL (FU/LIT)

Founded/First Service: April 1972/23 May 1972
Bases: Montpellier Méditerranée Airport, Mauguio, and Nice Airport, France
Services: Growing regional airline with an expanding network of domestic and cross-border routes. Points on the route system include Agen, Ajaccio, Avignon, Barcelona, Bergerac, Béziers, Biarritz, Bologna, Bordeaux, Clermont-Ferrand, Düsseldorf, Epinal, Florence, Frankfurt, Geneva, Lille, London, Lourdes/Tarbes, Lyon, Madrid, Manchester, Marseille, Milan, Nantes, Naples, Nice, Palermo, Paris, Pau, Périgueux, Perpignan, Quimper, Rimini, Rome, St Etienne, Strasbourg, Toulouse, Vannes, Venice and Verona. Air Littoral joined the Swissair-led Qualifier Group at the end of September 1998, when the SAir Group acquired a 44% shareholding. Existing franchises with Air France and Lufthansa may be terminated.
Fleet: 14 x ATR42-500, 17 x Bombardier (Canadair) CRJ-100ER, 5 x Fokker 70, 1 x Fokker 100.
On order: 2 x Bombardier (Canadair) CRJ-100ER
Colour Scheme: Air Littoral introduced a new corporate identity during 1996, to underscore its desire to redefine itself and its image as a 'company of the South'. The white fuselage is adorned with colourful designs in blue, yellow and red, including a striking interpretation of migratory birds flying against the blue skies, which cover the nose of the aircraft. Sun, stars, flowers and leaves are interwoven into a novel tail fin design. Unusually bold 'AIR LITTORAL' titles are painted at the rear of the fuselage in blue.
Illustrated: Bombardier (Canadair) CRJ-100ER.

AIR MALTA (KM/AMC)

Founded/First Service: 30 March 1973/1 April 1974
Base: Malta International Airport, Gudja, Malta
Services: National flag-carrier with an extensive network of scheduled passenger and cargo flights in Europe, and extending to North Africa and the Middle East, with a strong emphasis of tourist traffic to the Maltese islands. Destinations are Abu Dhabi, Amsterdam, Athens, Bahrain, Barcelona, Berlin, Birmingham, Brussels, Budapest, Cairo, Casablanca, Catania, Copenhagen, Damascus, Djerba, Dubai, Dublin, Düsseldorf, Frankfurt, Geneva, Glasgow, Gothenburg, Hamburg, Istanbul, Larnaca, Lisbon, London (Heathrow and Gatwick), Lyon, Manchester, Marseille, Milan, Monastir, Munich, Oslo, Palermo, Paris Orly, Rome, Rotterdam, Stockholm, Stuttgart, Tel Aviv, Tunis, Vienna and Zürich. An inter-island helicopter service, flown by Malta Air Charter, links Malta with the neighbouring island of Gozo.
Subsidiaries and Associates: Malta Air Charter (Gozo Wings) (100%), AZZURRAir (49%), Mediterranean Aviation (25%)
Fleet: 2 x Airbus A320-200, 2 x Boeing 737-200 Advanced, 5 x 737-300, 2 x 737-400
Malta Air Charter: 2 x Mil Mi-8P
Colour Scheme: The Air Malta corporate symbol is the eight-pointed, four-armed Maltese Cross, representing the four Christian values of prudence, justice, fortitude and temperance. It is displayed in white on a red field, covering the upper two thirds of the tail fin and underscored by three solid blue stripes, alluding to the three islands of Malta, Gozo and Comino. The three stripes are also carried along the fuselage right up to the nose of the aircraft. The Maltese Cross is repeated on the engines. The Air Malta logotype is applied in a Roman typeface. The present corporate identity was introduced in 1989.
Illustrated: Boeing 737-300

AIR MAURITIUS (MK/MAU)

Founded/First Service: 14 June 1967/August 1972
Base: Sir Seewoosagur Ramgoolam Airport, Plaine Magnien, Mauritius
Services: National airline providing international and regional flights within the Indian Ocean area and to Europe and the Far East. Destinations are Amsterdam (cargo only), Antananarivo, Brussels, Cape Town, Delhi, Durban, Frankfurt (joint service with Lufthansa), Geneva, Harare, Hong Kong (with Cathay Pacific), Jakarta, Johannesburg, Kuala Lumpur, London Heathrow and Gatwick, Mahé, Manchester, Melbourne, Moroni, Mumbai (with Air India), Munich (with Lufthansa), Nairobi, Paris, Perth, St Denis de la Réunion, Rodrigues, Rome, Singapore and Zürich. Flights within the island of Mauritius, mainly in support of tourism, are operated with Bell JetRanger helicopters.
Fleet: 5 x Airbus A340-300, 1 x ATR42-300, 2 x ATR42-500, 3 x Bell 206B JetRanger III, 2 x Boeing 767-200ER
On order: 1 x Airbus A340-300
Colour Scheme: A bright red windowline, trimmed below with a pinstripe in the same colour, runs the whole length of the aircraft, finished in white down to wing level. Upper case 'AIR MAURITIUS' titles are promoted alongside the national flag on the forward fuselage. The national flag, adopted on independence in 1968, features four colours: red for the martyrs of independence, blue for the sea, yellow for freedom, and green for its fertile soil. The airline's red Paille en Queu (a tropical bird) symbol flies across a white band on a quartered, largely red tail.
Illustrated: Airbus A340-300

AIR NAMIBIA (SW/NMB)

Founded/First Service: 1946 as South West Air Transport, present title adopted October 1991
Base: Eros and J. G. Strijdom airports, Windhoek, Namibia
Services: National airline maintaining a domestic and regional network of scheduled passenger and cargo services, together with long-haul flights from Windhoek to Frankfurt and London Heathrow. Local flights serve Cape Town, Johannesburg, Livingstone, Luanda, Lusaka, Maun and Victoria Falls, with domestic points, including the country's impressive tourist resorts, on the schedule including Keetmanshoop, Lüderitz, Mokuti Lodge, Mpacha, Ondangwa, Oranjemund, Swakopmund, Tsumeb, Walvis Bay and Windhoek.
Fleet: 1 x Boeing 737-200, 1 x 767-300ER, 3 x Beech 1900C
Colour Scheme: Namibia's national carrier introduced a new colour scheme with the delivery, in March 1998, of a Boeing 767-300ER. The tail fin is now essentially a representation of the national flag in blue, red, green and white, with the sun symbol, representing the country's ethnic groups, set into the blue field at the top of the fin. Retained is the 'straight through' yellow window line, framed by thinner blue lines top and bottom, on the otherwise white fuselage. Simple 'Air Namibia' titles are displayed in blue on the forward cabin roof. The airline's logo of a flamingo flying across a sun disk can be seen below the cheatlines with the words 'The National Airline of Namibia'.
Illustrated: Boeing 767-300ER

AIR NEW ZEALAND (NZ/ANZ)

Founded/First Service: 1939 as TEAL/30 April 1940, present name adopted 1 April 1965
Base: Auckland International Airport, Auckland, New Zealand
Services: National airline flying international flag services to and from Auckland, Wellington, Christchurch and Queenstown. The international network serves Apia, Frankfurt, Hong Kong, Honolulu, London, Los Angeles, Nadi, Nagoya, Norfolk Island, Noumea, Osaka, Papeete, Rarotonga, Singapore, Taipei, Tokyo and Tonga, and across the Tasman Sea to Brisbane, Cairns, Melbourne, Perth and Sydney, linking in with the domestic network of Ansett Australia, in which it has a 50% shareholding. Under codeshare agreements also offers flights to and from Boston, Chicago, Denver, Las Vegas, New York, San Francisco, Seattle, Toronto, Washington and Vancouver, and in the UK from Belfast, Edinburgh, Glasgow, Leeds/Bradford, Manchester and Teesside. Domestic services are provided to 26 towns and cities, plus feeder services under the *Air New Zealand Link* banner by Air Nelson and Eagle Airways. A strong tourist network is served, mainly on South Island, by Mount Cook Airline.
Subsidiaries and Associates: Ansett Australia (50%), Air Nelson (100%), Eagle Airways (100%), Mount Cook Line (100%)
Fleet: 10 x Boeing 737-200 Advanced, 1 x 737-200C Advanced, 5 x 747-200B, 7 x 747-400, 9 x 767-300ER, 4 x 767-200ER
On order: 7 x Boeing 737-300, 1 x 747-400.
Air Nelson: 6 x Fairchild SA227AC Metro III, 13 x Saab 340A. *Eagle Airways:* 9 x Embraer EMB-110P1 Bandeirante, 6 x Fairchild SA227AC Metro III. *Mount Cook:* 7 x ATR72-210, 9 x Cessna Skywagon, 3 x Pilatus PC-6/B2-H4 Turbo Porter. **On order for subsidiaries:** 7 x ATR72-500
Colour Scheme: The introduction of a bold new livery in April 1996 reflects the airline's desire to position itself as a world leader in air travel to and within the South Pacific. One of the key elements is the 'Pacific wave' in blue and turquoise, running through deep blue 'AIR NEW ZEALAND' titling on a clean white fuselage, symbolising the meeting of sea and shore around the islands of the Pacific. The deep blue tail fin bears in white a redesigned koru, the strong, curved spiral that dominated the beautifully etched canoe prows and signifies new life and replenishment.
Illustrated: Boeing 747-400

27

AIR ONE (AP/ADH)

Founded/First Service: 1983 as Aliadriatica, adopted present title April 1995
Bases: Rome Fiumicino (Leonardo da Vinci) and Milan airports, Italy
Services: Independent airline operating a domestic and European scheduled network and charter flights. European scheduled services are operated from Milan to Athens and London Stansted, with connecting services at Stansted to Aberdeen, Edinburgh and Glasgow with a partner airline, while the domestic network links Bari, Crotone, Naples, Reggio Calabria, Rome and Pescara.
Fleet: 3 x Boeing 737-200 Advanced, 4 x 737-300, 4 x 737-400,
2 x McDonnell Douglas DC-9-15F
Colour Scheme: Midnight blue and golden yellow are the dominant colours of the Air One corporate identity. Large blue elongated 'Air One' titles sit atop the windows on a white fuselage extending to below the wings, where the white gives way to grey paint. The letter 'O' in the title incorporates a yellow sun disk. Flying across the all-blue tail fin is a yellow flamingo, which is the company motif.
Illustrated: Boeing 737-400. *Alan J. Wright*

AIR SEYCHELLES (HM/SEY)

Founded/First Service: 15 September 1977 as Seychelles Airlines, present name adopted March 1979
Base: Seychelles International Airport, Victoria, Mahé, Seychelles
Services: National flag-carrier offering international passenger and cargo services from Mahé to Dubai, Frankfurt, Johannesburg, London Gatwick, Madrid, Manchester, Mauritius, Mumbai (Bombay), Nairobi, Paris Charles de Gaulle, Rome, Singapore and Zürich. Also provides domestic inter-island flights between Mahé, Praslin, Frégate, Bird, Denis and Desroches, serving the tourist industry. The main domestic shuttle provides more than 20 daily flights on the 15min Mahé-Praslin link.
Fleet: 1 x Boeing 767-200ER, 1 x 767-300ER, 4 x de Havilland Canada DHC-6 Twin Otter 300, 1 x Britten-Norman BN-2A Islander
Colour Scheme: A pair of pure white fairy terns flying in harmony against the background of the red and green colours of the Seychelles flag is the airline's symbol applied to the tail fin of its aircraft. The lower green is preceded by three graduated diagonal stripes wrapped over the top of the all-white fuselage. The symbol is also applied to the natural metal finish of the engine cowlings. Blue 'Air Seychelles' titles are displayed on the upper fuselage together with the national flag: its broad red band of revolution and progress and lower green alluding to its people's reliance on agriculture enclosing a white wavy stripe which symbolises the resources of the Indian Ocean where the islands are located.
Illustrated: Boeing 767-300ER

AIRTOURS INTERNATIONAL (VZ/AIH)

Founded/First Service: 1990/11 March 1991
Base: Manchester Airport, Manchester, United Kingdom
Services: Major UK charter airline providing inclusive tour services which cover most of the Mediterranean holiday resorts, as well as long-haul destinations in the Caribbean and the United States. Long-haul destinations include Antigua, Barbados, Grand Cayman, Orlando, Las Vegas, Honolulu, Montego Bay, St Kitts, Santo Domingo and Puerto Vallarta, as well as Banjul in West Africa and several regular points in Australia. Flights originate primarily from London Gatwick and Stansted, Birmingham, Cardiff, East Midlands, Glasgow, Liverpool, Manchester and Newcastle. The airline has introduced a new dimension in holiday flying, providing a choice of increased comfort and service in its new Premiair and Premiair Gold cabins. The Airtours Group now also includes Danish charter airline Premiair.
Fleet: 17 x Airbus A320-200, 2 x A321-200, 6 x Boeing 757-200, 4 x 767-300ER.
On order: 2 x Airbus A330-200
Premiair: 3 x Airbus A300B4-100, 6 x A320-200 (leased from Airtours), 2 x McDonnell Douglas DC-10-10
Colour Scheme: Airtours' aircraft are distinguished by a royal blue belly and tail fin, over a white fuselage, highlighted by a jade fuselage stripe and horizontal and vertical fin flashes in jade, orange and yellow, representing the group colours. The airline name appears in italicised royal blue lettering on the forward fuselage, with the Union flag above the first few cabin windows.
Illustrated: Airbus A330-200

Going further to make you happy

AIR TRANSAT (TS/TSC)

Founded/First Service: December 1986
Base: Montreal International Airport, Mirabel, Québec, Canada
Services: Canadian charter airline offering regular and ad hoc charter flights to the United States, Caribbean, Mexico, Central and South America, and across the Atlantic to Europe. European points served on a scheduled basis are Aberdeen, Amsterdam, Athens, Basel-Mulhouse, Belfast, Berlin, Birmingham, Bordeaux, Brussels, Cardiff, Dublin, Edinburgh, Exeter, Frankfurt, Glasgow, Leeds Bradford, Lisbon, London, Lyon, Manchester, Marseille, Nantes, Newcastle, Nice, Oporto, Palma de Mallorca, Paris, Ponta Delgada, Shannon, Terceira and Toulouse. Canadian cities on the schedule are Calgary, Edmonton, Gander, Halifax, Montreal, Québec City, St John's, Toronto, Vancouver and Whitehorse.
Fleet: 5 x Boeing 757-200, 2 x Lockheed L-1011-1 TriStar, 3 x L-1011-100 TriStar, 5 x L-1011-150 TriStar, 3 x L-1011-500 TriStar.
On order: 2 x Airbus A330-200
Colour Scheme: The Canadian charter airline introduced a smart new corporate identity during 1998. The dominant colour is a deeper royal blue, which offsets the glacier white of the fuselage. Set into the lower half of the royal blue tail fin is a sky blue five-pointed star with a white, fair weather cloud formation. Bold 'air transat' titles, also in royal blue, are painted across the forward windows and underscored by a red speed flash, which includes the airline's website: www.airtransat.com.
Illustrated: Lockheed L-1011-150
TriStar. *Terry Shone*

AIR ZIMBABWE (UM/AZW)

Founded/First Service: 1 September 1967 as Air Rhodesia, present title adopted in April 1980
Base: Harare Airport, Harare, Zimbabwe
Services: National flag-carrier providing long-haul services to Sydney via Perth, in conjunction with Qantas, and to European destinations including London Gatwick and Frankfurt via Larnaca. Also flies regional routes in Southern and East Africa serving Cape Town, Durban, Johannesburg, Gaborone, Manzini, Maputo, Lusaka, Nairobi, Lilongwe, Dar-es-Salaam, Mauritius and Windhoek. An eight-point domestic network incorporates Zimbabwe's main towns and particularly the country's famous tourist resorts. Points served are Bulawayo, Buffalo Range, Gweru, Harare, Hwange National Park, Kariba, Masvingo and Victoria Falls.
Fleet: 3 x Boeing 737-200 Advanced, 2 x 767-200ER, 1 x British Aerospace 146-200
Colour Scheme: A quadruple cheatline of the national colours of green, yellow, red and black on a white upper fuselage produces an exciting colour scheme. Commencing at the nose, the stripes step up in broader diagonal bands to the windowline, ultimately embracing most of the tail fin. Near the top of the fin appears the Zimbabwe bird, a soapstone carving of an ancient African culture, fronting the red star of socialism and national aspiration. 'air zimbabwe' titles in all-lower case are displayed alongside a fluttering portrayal of the national flag.
Illustrated: Boeing 767-200ER. *Alan J. Wright*

ALITALIA (AZ/AZA)

Founded/First Service: 16 September 1946/5 May 1947
Bases: Leonardo da Vinci Airport (Fiumicino), Rome, and Milan Malpensa Airport, Italy
Services: National airline providing international passenger and cargo services to more than 110 cities in 50 countries on all continents, with a strong emphasis on Europe, where it serves most major cities, and the Americas, linking Rome with Bogotá, Boston, Buenos Aires, Caracas, Chicago, Cleveland, Detroit, Houston, Lima, Los Angeles, Mexico City, Miami, Montreal, New York JFK and Newark, Philadelphia, Rio de Janeiro, San Francisco, Santiago de Chile, São Paulo, Toronto and Washington. Low-fare services are provided by Alitalia Team, while the airline's extensive domestic network is backed up by regional feeder flights operated by subsidiary Alitalia Express, formerly Avianova.
Subsidiaries and Associates: Alitalia Express (98%), Alitalia Team (100%), Eurofly (45%), Air Europe (27.5%)
Fleet: 19 x Airbus A321-100, 8 x Boeing 747-200B, 2 x 747-200F, 6 x 767-300ER, 3 x Boeing (McDonnell Douglas) MD-11, 5 x MD-11C, 90 x MD-82.
On order: 19 x Airbus A320-200, 6 x A321-100
Alitalia Express: 9 x ATR42-300, 4 x ATR72-210. *Alitalia Team:* 17 x Airbus A321-100, 6 x Boeing 767-300ER, 10 x Boeing (McDonnell Douglas) MD-82 (all leased from the mainline fleet).
Colour Scheme: Alitalia's striking corporate image in the national colours of red, white and green was designed by Walter Landor Associates and adopted fleetwide in January 1971. It focuses on a simple, yet bold stylised 'A' in green with a red centre, which fills the tail fin as a continuation of a green window line, fading to a point towards the nose. The 'A' is repeated as the first letter in the black italic logotype on the all-white fuselage.
Illustrated: Boeing (McDonnell Douglas) MD-11

ALLIANCE AIR (Y2/AFI)

Founded/First Service: 20 December 1994/1 July 1995
Base: Entebbe International Airport, Kampala, Uganda
Services: International carrier for Uganda and Tanzania, founded with the support of both countries' governments and national airlines, as well as South African Airways, which has a 40% stake. Long-haul routes are flown between Entebbe/Kampala, Dar-es-Salaam, Kilimanjaro and London Heathrow as well as to Mumbai (Bombay) in India. Associate Rwandan carrier, Alliance Express, operates between Kigali, Entebbe, Nairobi and Johannesburg.
Subsidiaries and Associates: Alliance Express (49%)
Fleet: 1 x Boeing 747SP, leased from South African Airways
Colour Scheme: A lion's head is drawn on and covers most of the tail fin, which is finished in a light burnt orange, reflecting the dry lands of the African bush. The colour rendition extends the length of the fuselage before fading out near the nose. The remainder of the aircraft is painted white. Darker orange-brown 'ALLIANCE' titles fill the space on the forward fuselage between the upper and main decks of the aircraft.
Illustrated: Boeing 747SP

ALL NIPPON AIRWAYS (ANA) (NH/ANH)

Founded/First Service: December 1957 through merger of JHAT and Far East Airlines
Bases: Tokyo Narita Airport, Tokyo, and Kansai International, Osaka, Japan
Services: Japan's largest airline with a comprehensive domestic network linking 35 cities on all Japanese islands with high-frequency services. Other points are served by subsidiary Air Nippon. International routes were introduced in 1986 and now serve Bangkok, Beijing, Brisbane, Dalian, Delhi, Denpasar (Bali), Frankfurt, Guam, Hong Kong, Honolulu, Jakarta, Kuala Lumpur, London Heathrow, Los Angeles, Milan, Moscow, Mumbai (Bombay), New York JFK, Qingdao, Paris, Rome, Saipan, Seoul, Shanghai, Singapore, Sydney, Tianjin, Vancouver, Vienna, Washington DC and Yangon.
Subsidiaries and Associates: Air Nippon (100%), Nippon Cargo Airlines (NCA) (14.1%), Austrian Airlines (9%)
Fleet: 17 x Airbus A320-200, 2 x A321-100, 5 x Boeing 747-200B, 20 x 747-400, 14 x 747SR, 22 x 767-200, 34 x 767-300, 8 x 767-300ER, 15 x 777-200, 4 x 777-300
On order: 4 x Airbus A321-100, 5 x A340-300, 2 x Boeing 747-400, 3 x 777-200, 4 x 777-300
Air Nippon: 8 x Airbus A320-200, 7 x Boeing 737-200 Advanced, 14 x 737-500, 2 x de Havilland Canada DHC-6 Twin Otter 300, 3 x NAMC YS-11A-500
Colour Scheme: An angular cheatline in two shades of blue broadens along the white upper fuselage until it takes over the whole of the tail, incorporating the 'ANA' logo in white. The logo also appears in Japanese on both sides of the fuselage near the front passenger door and is preceded by the hi-no-maru, or sun disk of the national flag. The livery was introduced in 1983 with the delivery of the Boeing 767s.
Illustrated: Boeing 767-200

ANA
All Nippon Airways

AMERICAN AIRLINES (AA/AAL)

Founded/First Service: 13 May 1934, predecessor companies go back to 15 April 1926
Base: Dallas/Fort Worth Airport, Fort Worth, Texas, USA
Services: World's largest airline, with an extensive domestic network from hubs at Dallas/Fort Worth, Chicago, Miami and San Juan right across America, including feeder services operated by its regional affiliate American Eagle. International schedules are also flown to Canada, Mexico, the Caribbean and Japan, and since 1982 across the Atlantic to Europe, now serving Amsterdam, Birmingham, Brussels, Frankfurt, Glasgow, London Heathrow, London Gatwick, Madrid, Manchester, Milan, Paris Orly, Stockholm and Zürich. A total of 165 cities are served on mainline schedules, with another 150 by American Eagle.
Subsidiaries and Associates: American Eagle (100%), Canadian Airlines International (33.3%)
Fleet: 35 x Airbus A300-600R, 78 x Boeing 727-200 Advanced, 97 x 757-200, 8 x 767-200, 22 x 767-200ER, 45 x 767-300ER, 11 x Boeing (McDonnell Douglas) MD-11, 250 x MD-82, 10 x MD-83, 75 x Fokker 100, 16 x McDonnell Douglas DC-10-10/ER, 4 x DC-10-30.
On order: 100 x Boeing 737-800, 5 x 757-200, 34 x 777-200ER
American Eagle: 46 x ATR42-300, 8 x ATR72-200, 23 x ATR72-210, 12 x ATR72-210A, 20 x Embraer ERJ-145, 108 x Saab 340B. **On order for subsidiary:** 25 x Bombardier (Canadair) CRJ-700, 22 x Embraer ERJ-145
Colour Scheme: A highly polished natural metal fuselage and tail finish provides the backdrop for a 'straight-through' patriotic triple cheatline in red, white and blue. The long-established motif of a blue eagle swoops down between the twin peaks of the double red and blue 'A' initials outlined in white. 'American' lettering in red, again with a white outline, is displayed on the cabin roof. The livery was adopted in 1969.
Illustrated: Boeing 757-200.

AMERICAN TRANS AIR (TZ/AMT)

Founded/First Service: 1973 as a Travel Club/March 1981
Base: Indianapolis International Airport, Indianapolis, Indiana, USA
Services: Holiday airline providing scheduled and charter service for leisure travellers, taking in Chicago, Dallas/Fort Worth, Denver, Fort Myers, Fort Lauderdale, Honolulu, Indianapolis, Las Vegas, Los Angeles, Maui (Hawaii), Miami, Milwaukee, New York, Orlando, Phoenix, Saint Petersburg, San Francisco, Sarasota, San Juan (Puerto Rico) and West Palm Beach. Additionally, American Trans Air has a strong charter-only business within the United States, to the Caribbean, and across the Atlantic to Europe.
Fleet: 24 x Boeing 727-200 Advanced, 8 x 757-200, 12 x Lockheed L-1011-50 TriStar, 2 x L-1011-100 TriStar
Colour Scheme: American Trans Air adopted a new colour scheme in early 1996 to identify itself more closely with its leisure business. Its largely white aircraft are now dominated by a painting-style tail fin, featuring a palm tree, bright sun, magenta waves and the airline initials on a mid-blue background. The underbelly is painted in the same blue, as are the engine cowlings, both decorated with similar motifs. Huge blue and gold 'ATA' initials cover the forward fuselage.
Illustrated: Lockheed L-1011 TriStar

AUSTRIAN AIRLINES (OS/AUA)

Founded/First Service: 30 September 1957/31 March 1958
Base: Vienna International Airport, Schwechat, Austria
Services: National airline providing scheduled passenger and cargo services to some 86 cities in 50 countries throughout Europe, and to the Middle and Far East, Africa and North America. Intercontinental destinations are Almaty, Aleppo, Amman, Atlanta, Beijing, Beirut, Cairo, Chicago, Damascus, Harare, Kathmandu, Johannesburg, Mauritius, New York, Osaka, Seoul, Singapore, Tehran, Tel Aviv, Tokyo and Washington. The network is further extended through its membership of the Swissair-led Qualifier alliance, other partnerships and through its equity stakes in Lauda Air and Tyrolean Airways. Austrian Air Transport (AAT) is a charter subsidiary using aircraft leased from the parent company as and when required.
Subsidiaries and Associates: Austrian Air Transport (AAT) (80%), Lauda Air (35.9%), Tyrolean Airways (100%), Ukraine International Airlines (18.4%)
Fleet: 4 x Airbus A310-300, 3 x A320-200, 5 x A321-100, 2 x A330-200, 2 x A340-200, 1 x A340-300, 7 x Boeing (McDonnell Douglas) MD-81, 6 x MD-82, 2 x MD-83, 2 x MD-87ER, 3 x MD-87SR
On order: 10 x Airbus A320-200, 2 x A321-100, 2 x A330-200, 1 x A340-300
Colour Scheme: Austrian Airlines launched the first major redesign of its livery on 4 October 1995. Designed by GGK Vienna and UK consultants Davies and Barron, the scheme connects the national colour scheme of red, white and red on the tail fin, with the colours of the Austrian landscape. These are the green of the woods and meadows, and the blue of rivers and lakes, achieved by a blue/green colour line under the windows. The famous red arrow symbol provides an element of continuity, and is set into the centre of the tail and ahead of anthracite grey 'AUSTRIAN AIRLINES' titles. The aircraft is otherwise painted in Alpine white, suggesting the country's snow-covered mountains and icy glaciers.
Illustrated: Fokker 70

AUSTRIAN AIRLINES ➤

AVIANCA (AV/AVA)

Founded/First Service: 5 December 1919/12 September 1920 as SCADTA, adopted present title 14 June 1940

Base: Eldorado International Airport, Bogotá, Colombia

Services: National flag-carrier operating an extensive domestic network and scheduled flights throughout Latin America, the Caribbean, the United States and Europe. Destinations include Buenos Aires, Caracas, Frankfurt, Guatemala City, Havana, Lima, London Heathrow, Los Angeles, Madrid, Mexico City, Miami, Montego Bay, New York JFK and Newark, Panama City, Paris CDG, Quito, Rio de Janeiro, San José, São Paulo and Santiago de Chile. Further domestic services, together with flights to Aruba, Curaçao and Panama City, are scheduled by subsidiary SAM.

Subsidiaries and Associates: SAM Colombia (94%), Helicol (100%)

Fleet: 3 x Boeing 727-200 Advanced, 4 x 757-200, 3 x 767-200ER, 1 x 767-300ER, 11 x Boeing (McDonnell Douglas) MD-83, 10 x Fokker 50

SAM: 9 x British Aerospace (Avro) RJ100

Colour Scheme: The upper half of the fuselage is painted in a warm red, falling away from a complete coverage at the nose to above the window line at the rear and continuing up the back of the tail. Red 'Avianca' lettering colours the white section of the fin. 'Avianca Colombia' titles are set into the red field ahead of the wing in white and black respectively.

Illustrated: Boeing 757-200

BALKAN BULGARIAN AIRLINES (LZ/LAZ)

Founded/First Service: 29 June 1947/12 September 1947 as TABSO, present title adopted in 1968

Base: Sofia International Airport, Sofia, Bulgaria

Services: National flag-carrier operating domestic and international passenger and cargo services to points in Europe, North America, Africa and the Middle and Far East. Destinations served from Sofia include Accra, Algiers, Amsterdam, Ankara, Athens, Bahrain, Bangkok, Beirut, Belgrade, Berlin, Brussels, Bucharest, Budapest, Cairo, Casablanca, Copenhagen, Damascus, Dubai, Frankfurt, Helsinki, Istanbul, Kiev, Kuwait, Lagos, Larnaca, London Heathrow, Madrid, Malta, Milan, Moscow, New York JFK, Paris CDG, Prague, Rome, St Petersburg, Stockholm, Tirana, Tel Aviv, Tunis, Vienna, Warsaw and Zürich. Domestic services link Sofia, Bourgas and Varna. Balkan Bulgarian Airlines also undertakes charter and Hadj flights.

Fleet: 3 x Antonov An-12, 6 x An-24V, 3 x Boeing 737-500, 2 x 767-200ER, 1 x Ilyushin IL-18D, 1 x IL-18V, 7 x Tupolev Tu-154B-1/2, 8 x Tu-154M

Colour Scheme: Narrow twin cheatlines in the national colours of red and mid-green flow along the pure white fuselage, wrapping around the belly of the aircraft behind the wing. Red and green brush strokes on the white tail add a fresh, modern look. Bold red 'Balkan' titles are applied in English on the starboard side and Bulgarian on port, midway on the cabin roof behind the 'shooting star' emblem. These are followed by smaller 'Bulgarian Airlines' subtitles in green. The present scheme was adopted in late 1985.

Illustrated: Boeing 767-200ER. *Alan J. Wright*

BIMAN BANGLADESH AIRLINES (BG/BBC)

Founded/First Service: 4 January 1972/February 1972
Base: Zia International Airport, Dhaka, Bangladesh
Services: National airline operating scheduled international flag services from the capital Dhaka to 27 destinations in 21 countries. Cities served include Abu Dhabi, Bahrain, Bangkok, Brussels, Calcutta, Delhi, Doha, Dubai, Frankfurt, Hong Kong, Jeddah, Karachi, Kathmandu, Kuala Lumpur, Kuwait, London Heathrow, Mumbai (Bombay), Muscat, New York JFK, Paris CDG, Rome, Singapore, Tokyo and Yangon. Also serves a domestic flight network serving nine points, including Barisal, Chittagong, Cox's Bazaar, Dhaka, Ishurdi, Jessore, Rajshahi, Saidpur and Sylhet.
Fleet: 2 x Airbus A310-300, 2 x British Aerospace ATP, 2 x Fokker F28-4000 Fellowship, 4 x McDonnell Douglas DC-10-30
Colour Scheme: The national colours of red and dark green are used in the form of a cheatline running at window level the whole length of the all-white fuselage, cut to a fine point at the front. Dark green 'BANGLADESH AIRLINES' titles are carried in English and Bengali on the port and starboard side respectively, preceded by the national flag. A white stork, flying across the rising sun represented by a crimson disk, is positioned centrally between horizontal fin bands in red and green, and on the engine cowlings. The livery was introduced in 1983 with the delivery of the DC-10s.
Illustrated: Airbus A310-300

বাংলাদেশ বিমান Bangladesh Biman

BRAATHENS (BU/BRA)

Founded/First Service: 26 March 1946 as Braathens SAFE/December 1946, adopted present name in March 1998

Base: Oslo-Gardermoen Airport, Oslo, Norway

Services: Biggest domestic operator in Norway, serving 14 major towns and cities, including Alesund, Bergen, Bodo, Harstad/Narvik, Haugesund, Kristiansand, Kristiansund, Molde, Oslo, Roros, Stavanger, Svalbard (Spitzbergen), Tromso and Trondheim, with operations centred at Oslo, Stavanger, Bergen and Trondheim. International schedules link Oslo with Alicante, Amsterdam, Billund, Jersey, London Stansted, Malaga, Milan, Murmansk, Newcastle and Stockholm. Braathens, owned 30% by KLM, is a partner of the KLM/Northwest alliance. Braathens Sweden (formerly Transwede) and Malmö Aviation operate in the Swedish domestic market, from Stockholm to Malmo in the south and Lulea in the north.

Subsidiaries and Associates: Braathens Sweden (100%), Malmö Aviation (100%)

Fleet: 7 x Boeing 737-400, 20 x 737-500, 3 x 737-700.

On order: 5 x 737-700.

Braathens Sweden: 1 x Boeing 737-500, 4 x Fokker 100. ***Malmö Aviation:*** 11 x British Aerospace 146-200

Colour Scheme: The airline changed its livery and simplified its name in March 1998. The new motif in the shape of a stylised, modern wing, is a symbol of its transformation into an airline of the next century, ready for the new opportunities in Scandinavia and on a global basis. The aircraft fuselage is painted in light grey with a deep blue stripe surrounded by a red border. The stripe runs the whole length of the aircraft and ends in a 'dancing' Northern lights pattern on the tail fin. The Norwegian flag, previously on the tail fin, has been moved to a more prominent position on both sides of the cockpit windows. The Northern lights, which can be seen in large parts of Scandinavia on clear winter nights, are a prominent feature of the new livery and underline Braathens' connection with the northern countries.

Illustrated: Boeing 737-500. *Kajetan Steiner*

BRIT AIR (DB/BZH)

Founded/First Service: 1973
Base: Aérodrome de Ploujean, Morlaix, Brittany, France
Services: Major French regional airline providing scheduled services within Metropolitan France and to neighbouring countries, both in its own right and as an *Air France Express* partner. Its route network covers 20 cities in its home country, plus 15 elsewhere in Europe, including Barcelona, Brussels, Cologne/Bonn, Düsseldorf, Geneva, Hamburg, London Gatwick, Madrid, Milan, Munich, Rome, Southampton, Stuttgart, Vienna and Zürich. French cities served are Caen, Bordeaux, Brest, Clermont-Ferrand, Deauville, Le Havre, Lille, Limoges, Lyon, Marseille, Nantes, Nice, Paris CDG and Orly, Quimper, Rennes, Rouen, Strasbourg and Toulouse.
Fleet: 10 x ATR42-300, 2 x ATR72-200, 14 x Bombardier (Canadair) CRJ-100ER.
On order: 5 x Bombardier (Canadair) CRJ-100ER, 2 x CRJ-700
Colour Scheme: Brit Air's corporate identity provides a clean modern look, highlighted by an overall white fuselage, 'BRIT AIR' titles in European blue near the front and on the engine cowlings, and the company motif applied on the vertical tail fin and, on a smaller scale, below the rear cockpit window. The motif comprises two parts: *Triskele*, a Celtic symbol representing the three elements of earth, fire and water, and *Hermine*, the emblem of Brittany. Colours were selected from the region's natural environment, including the yellow broom for Triskele, the white of the Breton flag as the main colour of the aircraft, and European blue for Hermine and the airline's titles.
Illustrated: Bombardier (Canadair) CRJ-700.
Bombardier Regional Aircraft/Aerospace

BRITANNIA AIRWAYS (BY/BAL)

Founded/First Service: 1 December 1961/5 May 1962 as Euravia (London), present title adopted 16 August 1964

Base: London Luton Airport, Luton, Bedfordshire, United Kingdom

Services: World's biggest charter airline providing inclusive-tour flights from Luton, London Gatwick, Manchester, Birmingham and some 14 other provincial UK airports to more than 100 regular destinations throughout Europe and the Mediterranean countries, taking in all the main holiday resort areas of Portugal, Spain, Italy, Greece, Turkey, Tunisia, Malta and the Canary Islands. Also operates long-haul routes to such destinations as the Maldives, India, Thailand, Australia, New Zealand, Mexico, Canada, the United States, and the Caribbean. Expansion into the German and Scandinavian holiday market was effected in November 1997 with the launch of German subsidiary, Britannia GmbH, followed in February 1998 by the takeover of Blue Scandinavia, now renamed Britannia AB.

Subsidiaries and Associates: Britannia AB (100%), Britannia GmbH (100%)

Fleet: 19 x Boeing 757-200, 5 x 757-200ER, 6 x 767-200ER, 9 x 767-300ER

On order: 5 x 737-800

Colour Scheme: A patriotic livery with deep-blue full-length stripes beginning at the belly of the aircraft and graduating to a pinstripe as they approach the window line. The blue is trimmed with narrow red and gold bands. The white upper fuselage displays strong 'Britannia' lettering and Queen Boadicea's helmeted head in blue outlined in red. The warrior queen, carrying a trident and holding the Union flag shield, sits on the blue tail above reversed pinstripes. The livery was created by London design house Peter Eaton & Partners and implemented in 1983.

Illustrated: Boeing 767-300

BRITISH AIRWAYS (BA/BAW)

Founded/First Service: 31 March 1924 as Imperial Airways, present title adopted 1 April 1972
Bases: London Heathrow and Gatwick airports, United Kingdom
Services: Major British airline operating the largest global network of scheduled passenger and cargo services linking the UK with more than 180 destinations in 80 countries on all continents. Also comprehensive domestic network including the main 'Super Shuttle' services from London to Manchester, Glasgow, Edinburgh and Belfast, the Scottish Highlands and Islands routes and regional flights. The network is further extended through the recently formed *'oneworld'* global alliance, which also includes American Airlines, Canadian Airlines International, Cathay Pacific Airways and Qantas, many other partnerships, and through a growing list of franchise operations in the UK, Denmark and South Africa, which add another 75 destinations in British Airways colours.
Subsidiaries and Associates: Air Liberté (67%), Brymon Airways (100%), Deutsche BA (100%), Go (100%), CityFlyer Express (100%), Qantas (25%), Air Mauritius (12.8%). *Franchises:* British Mediterranean Airways, British Regional Airlines, Comair (South Africa), GB Airways, Loganair, Maersk Air UK and Sun-Air of Scandinavia (Denmark)
Fleet: 7 x Aérospatiale/BAC Concorde, 10 x Airbus A320-200, 30 x Boeing 737-200, 4 x 737-300, 34 x 737-400, 15 x 747-100, 13 x 747-200B, 3 x 747-200(SCD), 46 x 747-400, 51 x 757-200, 28 x 767-300ER, 6 x 777-200, 13 x 777-200ER, 10 x British Aerospace ATP, 8 x McDonnell Douglas DC-10-30 (to be withdrawn during 1999).
On order: 39 x Airbus A319-100,20 x A320-200, 6 x Boeing 747-400, 6 x 757-200, 26 x 777-200ER
Air Liberté: 3 x ATR42-300, 2 x ATR72-200, 9 x Boeing (McDonnell Douglas) MD-83, 4 x Fokker F28-2000 Fellowship, 10 x Fokker 100, 3 x McDonnell Douglas DC-10-30. *Brymon Airways:* 10 x Bombardier DHC-8-300, 2 x de Havilland Canada DHC-7-110. *CityFlyer Express:* 6 x ATR42-300, 5 x ATR72-200, 5 x British Aerospace (Avro) RJ100. **On order for subsidiary:** 2 x Avro RJ100. *Deutsche BA:* 20 x Boeing 737-300. **On order for subsidiary:** 2 x Boeing 737-300. *Go:* 8 x Boeing 737-300

Colour Scheme: British Airways launched its long-awaited and revolutionary new corporate identity on 10 June 1997, created by London design consultancy Newell and Sorrell. Said to depict British Airways as a global, caring company, more modern, more open, more cosmopolitan, but proud of its 'Britishness', the airline has turned its aircraft into a flying art gallery with designs from around the world. The process is far from complete but the majority of the 50 planned images can now be seen on the tail fins of the BA aircraft. At the same time, British Airways introduced a brighter and lighter corporate palette of red, white and blue, drawn more closely from the Union flag. The airline name is applied in a new softer, rounder typeface, and the flat red speedwing symbol was evolved into a new three-dimensional Speedmarque. Both are applied in a large format on the front fuselage, which is white above wing level and blue below. The only exception is Concorde, which is painted all in white and features a fluttering adaptation of the Union flag on the tail.

Illustrated: Close-up of Concorde tail, Boeing 747-400, Aérospatiale/BAC Concorde, Boeing 737-300 (Go), British Airways (Maersk) Bombardier (Canadair) CRJ-200LR

BRITISH MIDLAND (BD/BMA)

Founded/First Service: 1938 as Air Schools, present title adopted 1964
Base: East Midlands Airport, Castle Donington, Derbyshire, United Kingdom
Services: Major UK independent airline operating scheduled passenger flights to 12 domestic destinations and the Channel Islands, and European services to Amsterdam, Bergen, Brussels, Cologne/Bonn, Copenhagen, Dresden, Düsseldorf, Esbjerg, Faro, Frankfurt, Malaga, Nice, Oslo, Palma de Mallorca, Paris, Prague and Warsaw. Many destinations are served from London Heathrow, where the airline is the second-largest carrier after British Airways. Long-haul transatlantic flights are under consideration. Feeder services are provided by Scottish airline Business Air, now trading as British Midland Commuter.
Subsidiaries and Associates: British Midland Commuter (100%)
Fleet: 4 x Airbus A320, 8 x Boeing 737-300, 5 x 737-400, 12 x 737-500, 6 x Fokker 100, 3 x Fokker 70.
On order: 18 x Airbus A320/A321
British Midland Commuter: 7 x Saab 340A, 3 x Saab 340B. **On order for subsidiary:** 10 x Embraer ERJ-145
Colour Scheme: British Midland unveiled an update of its products and aircraft livery on 30 September 1996. Midnight blue and red cheatlines now separate the pale grey underside of the aircraft from the deep blue cabin roof. New 'British Midland' titles in white upper and lower case lettering are applied alongside the red 'BM' motif, which is partially striated to give the appearance of speed. The 'M' is crowned with a white diamond, alluding to the airline's inflight Diamond service. The words 'The Airline for Europe' have also been added. The 'BM' motif dominates the tail fin as before.
Illustrated: Airbus A321

BWIA INTERNATIONAL (BW/BWA)

Founded/First Service: 27 November 1939
Base: Piarco Airport, Port of Spain, Trinidad and Tobago
Services: National carrier providing passenger and cargo flights throughout the Caribbean islands, to South America, North America, and across the North Atlantic. Destinations in the Caribbean are Antigua, Barbados, Grenada, Jamaica, St Lucia and St Maarten, plus the short hops across to Caracas, Venezuela and Georgetown, Guyana on the South American continent. The Caribbean is also linked with New York, Miami, Toronto and London on direct daily flights.
Fleet: 4 x Lockheed L-1011-500 TriStar, 5 x Boeing (McDonnell Douglas) MD-83
Colour Scheme: BWIA has initiated a corporate rebranding and image makeover, which is due to be completed by May 1999. Its new corporate identity comprises a golden 'sand' cheatline above a Caribbean blue pinstripe sky. The golden cheatline fills most of the tail fin and is interrupted only by the airline's steelpan symbol in turquoise and gold, itself broken by magenta 'BWIA' initials. 'BWIA International' titles cover the forward fuselage, ahead of the national flag and the words 'We are the Caribbean'. Lettering is black with the exception of the initials, which are again in magenta. The steelpan is the country's national instrument, and is said to be the only new musical instrument to be invented this century.
Illustrated: Lockheed L-1011-500 TriStar

CALEDONIAN AIRWAYS (KT/BKT)

Founded/First Service: 10 December 1987
Bases: London Gatwick Airport, Gatwick, West Sussex, United Kingdom
Services: Operates in the charter market, offering holiday flights to the traditional
Mediterranean resort and year-round long-haul flights to destinations as far afield as
Barbados, the United States, Kenya, Goa and the Maldives. All the popular sunspots in Spain,
Greece, Portugal and Turkey are served in the summer programme. During winter, the
European operation switches to the ski slopes of the Alps and Pyrenees. Operations at the
cheaper end of the Mediterranean market are flown by its low-cost Peach Air brand.
Fleet: 5 x Airbus A320-200, 5 x Lockheed L1011 TriStar 100, 2 x McDonnell Douglas DC-10-30
Colour Scheme: The Caledonian Airways fleet combines the best of both British Airways and
the former British Caledonian Airways, although now owned by the Thomas Cook Group. The
fuselage features a pearl-grey upper and midnight blue underside of the aircraft, highlighted
by a gold cheat line set into the blue in mid-fuselage. The midnight blue tail fin displays the
familiar lion rampant in gold. Blue 'CALEDONIAN' titles in an Optima typeface are displayed
on the forward cabin roof.
Illustrated: Airbus A320

CANADIAN AIRLINES (CP/CDN)

Founded/First Service: January 1987 through merger of CP Air, Pacific Western Airlines, Nordair and Eastern Provincial Airways

Base: Calgary, Toronto and Vancouver International Airports, Canada

Services: Canadian Airlines operates Canada's largest domestic network, together with regional and long-haul flights to 30 destinations in 18 countries serving Auckland, Bangkok, Beijing, Boston, Buenos Aires, Chicago O'Hare, Dallas/Fort Worth, Frankfurt, Hong Kong, Honolulu, Kingston, Lima, London Heathrow, Los Angeles, Mexico City, Miami, Nagoya, Nadi, New York LaGuardia, Orlando, Paris, Rio de Janeiro, Rome, Santiago de Chile, São Paulo, Seattle, Sydney, Taipei, Tokyo and Washington. The airline is part of the British Airways-led 'oneworld' alliance, which also includes American Airlines, Cathay Pacific and Qantas. The domestic network is enhanced through a number of local airlines, which operate as a Canadian Partner/Partner Canadien in Canadian Airlines International colours.

Subsidiaries and Associates: *Canadian Partner:* Air Alma, Air Atlantic, Air Georgian, Canadian Regional Airlines, Inter-Canadien (1991) and Pacific Coastal Airlines

Fleet: 12 x Airbus A320-200, 43 x Boeing 737-200 Advanced, 4 x 747-400, 11 x 767-300ER, 5 x McDonnell Douglas DC-10-30, 5 x DC-10-30ER.

On order: 10 x Airbus A320-200

Colour Scheme: The key element of the new 'Proud Wings' corporate identity is a contemporary rendition of the Canada goose, which flies from the tail fin of its aircraft. The symbol was chosen because it is part of the country's natural heritage and because its characteristics are said to mirror the values of Canadian Airlines. The teamwork, sharing of responsibilities and support for customers, colleagues and communities is symbolised by the instincts of Canada geese: flying in formation, rotating the lead position and encouraging leaders to keep up their speed. The airline has retained the white cabin roof and Pacific blue underside of the aircraft, separated by a red pinstripe. Red 'Canadian' titles are applied ahead of the wing, with the penultimate character replaced by an arrow, so that it can be read as either 'Canadian' or the French 'Canadien', without having to apply dual titling.

Illustrated: Boeing 747-400. *Cohn & Wolfe*

CARGOLUX AIRLINES INTERNATIONAL (CV/CLX)

Founded/First Service: 4 March 1970

Base: Luxembourg (Findel) Airport, Grand Duchy of Luxembourg

Services: One of Europe's leading cargo-only airlines, operating regular scheduled services between Europe, the Americas, the Near and Middle East, Africa and Asia Pacific, together with worldwide charter flights. Among regular destinations are Abu Dhabi, Bangkok, Beirut, Chennai (Madras), Colombo, Damascus, Dubai, Hong Kong, Houston, Istanbul, Johannesburg, Keflavik, Komatsu, Kuala Lumpur, Kuwait, Los Angeles, Mexico City, Miami, New York, San Francisco, Santiago de Chile, São Paulo, Seattle, Singapore and Taipei. Also offers maintenance and sub-leasing services, as well as CHAMP (Cargo Handling and Management Planning), the only fully integrated cargo system in the world.

Fleet: 6 x Boeing 747-400F.

On order: 4 x Boeing 747-400F, plus two options

Colour Scheme: The light-grey-painted overall fuselage is highlighted by simple straight cheatlines using the blue, white and red tricolour of Luxembourg, broken on the forward fuselage by bold black 'cargolux' titling in lower case lettering. The airline's distinctive three-dimensional 'triple box' motif in red outlined in white dominates the aircraft's massive tail fin. On the 747-400F, the motif is also reproduced on the aircraft's distinctive winglets.

Illustrated: Boeing 747-400F. *Paul Mirgain and Georges Huberty*

CATHAY PACIFIC AIRWAYS (CX/CPA)

Founded/First Service: 24 September 1946
Base: Hong Kong International Airport, Chek Lap Kok, Hong Kong, China
Services: Major privately-owned Hong Kong airline operating scheduled passenger and cargo services to 47 destinations in Australia, New Zealand, the Middle and Far East, Europe, Africa and North America. Another 18 cities are served within China through its associate Dragonair, which also provides regional services within Asia. Cathay's long-haul intercontinental flights serve Adelaide, Amsterdam, Auckland, Bahrain, Brisbane, Cairns, Christchurch, Dubai, Frankfurt, Johannesburg, London Heathrow, Los Angeles, Manchester, Melbourne, New York, Paris CDG, Perth, Rome, Sydney, Toronto, Vancouver and Zürich. Other destinations are served through its participation in the British Airways-led *'oneworld'* alliance and other partnership arrangements. The airline also has a strong cargo business, which is further enhanced through its majority ownership in all-cargo airline, AHK-Air Hong Kong.
Subsidiaries and Associates: AHK-Air Hong Kong (75%), Dragonair (Hong Kong Dragon Airlines) (20%)
Fleet: 12 x Airbus A330-300, 11 x A340-300, 7 x Boeing 747-200B, 4 x 747-200F, 6 x 747-300, 19 x 747-400, 2 x 747-400F, 4 x 777-200, 4 x 777-300.
On order: 3 x Boeing 777-300
AHK-Air Hong Kong: 3 x Boeing 747-200F
Colour Scheme: Centrepiece of the Landor Associates-designed identity is the 'brushwing' — a calligraphy stroke suggesting the wing of a bird — against a green background taking up most of the tail fin, and appearing in a similar arrangement under the cockpit. A red 'speed bar' encloses the bottom of the logo. The brushwing has been chosen to symbolise modern energy and confident elegance, representing the airline's well-won reputation for technical excellence and exacting standards of service. Together with the green 'CATHAY PACIFIC' titling based on the arrow style on the shoulder of the aircraft, the image is said to have an oriental feel, while appealing to both its Asian and Western customers. The fuselage is largely grey, with a white roof from wing level.
Illustrated: Airbus
A340-300

CHANNEL EXPRESS (LA/EXS)

Founded: January 1978 as Express Air Services, adopted present title in 1982
Base: Bournemouth International Airport, Christchurch, Dorset, United Kingdom
Services: All-cargo airline operating daily scheduled cargo flights between Bournemouth and the Channel Islands, together with general *ad hoc* cargo charter flights throughout Europe and to North Africa, including the carriage of newspapers and vehicle parts. Contract mail flights are provided for the Royal Mail and Parcelforce to Bristol, Coventry, East Midlands, Edinburgh, Liverpool, London Gatwick, Luton and Newcastle. Other express services are flown for leading overnight parcels companies and international airlines within the UK and to European destinations. The large Airbus freighters in its fleet enable Channel Express to offer supplemental cargo services to major airlines throughout Europe, Africa, and the Middle and Far East.
Fleet: 3 x Airbus A300B4-100F, 5 x Fokker F27-500 Friendship, 3 x F27-600,
4 x Lockheed L-188C Electra
Colour Scheme: The white overall aircraft is finished by a bright green tail fin, which wraps around the rear fuselage. 'channel express' titles in two-tone green appear on the forward fuselage and reversed out in white on the tail fin, with the first letter 'n' carrying the Rose of Sarnia, the symbol of the Bailiwick of Guernsey, the second-largest of the Channel Islands lying off the northern coast of France. The word 'express' is graduated to give an impression of speed.
Illustrated: Airbus A300B4-100F

CHINA AIRLINES (CI/CAL)

Founded: 16 December 1959
Base: Chiang Kai-Shek International Airport, Taipei, Taiwan
Services: Taiwan's flag-carrier providing regional and international passenger services from Taipei to 29 cities, including Abu Dhabi, Amsterdam, Anchorage, Bangkok, Denpasar (Bali), Frankfurt, Fukuoka, Hanoi, Ho Chi Minh City, Hong Kong, Honolulu, Jakarta, Kuala Lumpur, Los Angeles, Manila, Nagoya, New York, Okinawa, Phuket, Rome, San Francisco, Singapore, Sydney, Tokyo, Vancouver and Zürich. Subsidiary Mandarin Airlines uses aircraft leased from the parent company on services to Brisbane and Sydney in Australia. Domestic services are flown from Taipei to Kaohsiung. China Airlines also provides all-cargo flights to 17 destinations. The regional and domestic network is further extended through its part ownership in smaller local airlines.
Subsidiaries and Associates: Mandarin Airlines (100%), Formosa Airlines (42%), Far Eastern Air Transport (10%)
Fleet: 12 x Airbus A300-600R, 6 x A300B4-200, 3 x Boeing 737-200 Advanced, 3 x 747-200B(SCD), 8 x 747-200F, 12 x 747-400, 2 x 747SP, 5 x Boeing (McDonnell Douglas) MD-11. **On order:** 2 x Boeing 737-800, 1 x 747-400
Colour Scheme: The present corporate identity, introduced on 7 October 1995, was developed by Singaporean consultancy Addison Design, to illustrate the airline's commitment to sincerity, caring, innovation, sense of responsibility and the pursuit of excellence. The essence of the scheme is the pink plum blossom, the national flower of Taiwan, which adorns the tail fin of the aircraft, floating on a purple haze. The otherwise all-white aircraft features a two-tone blue chinstrap, with the upper lighter shade extending to the rear on the underside of the fuselage. Blue 'CHINA AIRLINES' titles are applied forward (on the Boeing 747 between the upper and main decks), with an abbreviated form in Chinese characters.
Illustrated: Airbus A300-600

CHINA EASTERN AIRLINES (MU/CES)

Founded/First Service: 25 June 1988
Base: Hongqiao International Airport, Shanghai, People's Republic of China
Services: One of the largest air enterprises in China, serving a trunk network of domestic routes to some 45 cities from its main base at Shanghai, and from regional centres at Hefei City, Nanchang, Nanjing and Qingdao. The airline also operates a fast-expanding regional network, together with long-haul routes to Europe and the United States, which presently serve Bangkok, Brussels, Chicago, Fukuoka, Los Angeles, Madrid, Munich, Nagasaki, Nagoya, Osaka, Pusan, San Francisco, Seattle, Seoul, Singapore, Sydney and Tokyo. China Eastern is also responsible for general aviation services, such as agricultural spraying and survey work.
Fleet: 10 x Airbus A300-600R, 5 x A340-300, 3 x Antonov An-24V, 2 x Boeing 737-300, 5 x Boeing (McDonnell Douglas) MD-11, 1 x MD-11F, 13 x MD-82, 7 x MD-90-30, 10 x Fokker 100, 20 x Shijazhuang Y5, 4 x Xian Y7, 3 x Y7-100.
On order: 7 x Airbus A320-200, 2 x Boeing (McDonnell Douglas) MD-90-30
Colour Scheme: China Eastern's aircraft are painted in white and grey, separated by red and blue cheat lines enclosing a golden pencil line. The cheat lines are wrapped around the nose and rear fuselage. 'CHINA EASTERN' titles are applied on the mid-fuselage roof, in red Chinese characters and blue English wording. The tail fin is dominated by a red sun rising from a blue sea, through which flies a white stylised bird at dawn.
Illustrated: Airbus A320-200

CONDOR FLUGDIENST (DE/CFG)

Founded/First Service: 21 December 1955/28 March 1956 as Deutsche Flugdienst, present name adopted 25 October 1961

Base: Frankfurt Rhein/Main Airport, Frankfurt, Germany

Services: Germany's leading holiday airline, providing inclusive-tour services to more than 50 destinations in 34 countries. In addition to short-haul flights to the Mediterranean basin, Condor is expanding its long-haul operations, which currently serve the resort areas in the Caribbean and Central America, East Africa and the Far East. Typical long-haul destinations are Antigua, Bangkok, Barbados, Cancun, Colombo, Fort Lauderdale, Kilimanjaro, Maldives, Mauritius, Montego Bay, Nassau, Phuket, Puerto Plata, Punta Cana, Puerto Vallarta, San Juan, Santo Domingo, Seychelles, Tampa, Tobago and Varadero. Flights originate at all major German airports, but principally from Frankfurt, Berlin, Cologne/Bonn, Hannover and Munich.

Subsidiaries and Associates: Condor Berlin (100%), SunExpress Airlines (40%)

Fleet: 5 x Airbus A320-200, 4 x Boeing 737-300, 18 x 757-200, 9 x 767-300ER, 3 x Boeing (McDonnell Douglas) DC-10-30

On order: 3 x Airbus A320-200, 13 x Boeing 757-300

Colour Scheme: As a member of the Lufthansa Group, Condor also uses the corporate colours of blue and yellow, but in reverse. Its aircraft sport a yellow tail fin and a stylised bird symbol enclosed in a circle, both in blue, and large 'Condor' titles on the forward fuselage in a matching blue Helvetica typeface. The aircraft body is painted in pristine white, with only the underside below wing level finished in yellow. The tail design is repeated on the engine cowlings, while the company symbol also appears under the side cockpit window. The Berlin-based subsidiary also has the word 'Berlin' in grey above the rear of the title.

Illustrated: Airbus A320-200

CONTINENTAL AIRLINES (CO/COA)

Founded: 15 July 1934 as Varney Speed Lines, present title adopted 1 July 1937
Bases: Houston Intercontinental Airport, Texas, and New York Newark, USA
Services: One of the world's major airlines with an extensive network of scheduled passenger flights, serving 125 US cities and 67 international destinations, extended further through a number of major global alliances. Another 81 smaller cities in the US and Canada are served by regional subsidiary, Continental Express, linking into its hubs at Houston, Newark and Cleveland. In Europe, Continental is the second-largest US carrier in terms of cities served, providing onward connections at the US hubs from Birmingham, Brussels, Dublin, Düsseldorf, Frankfurt, Glasgow, Lisbon, London Gatwick, Madrid, Manchester, Milan, Paris Charles de Gaulle, Rome, Shannon and Zürich. Continental Micronesia operates in five markets in the Western Pacific from its base at Guam, using aircraft leased from the parent company.
Subsidiaries and Associates: Continental Express (100%), Continental Micronesia (50%)
Fleet: 43 x Boeing 727-200 Advanced, 4 x 737-100, 15 x 727-200, 65 x 737-300, 66 x 737-500, 15 x 737-700, 2 x 737-800, 4 x 747-200B, 28 x 757-200, 5 x Boeing (McDonnell Douglas) MD-81, 56 x MD-82, 8 x MD-83, 28 x McDonnell Douglas DC-9-30, 34 x DC-10-30.
On order: 2 x Boeing 737-500, 33 x 737-700, 30 x 737-800, 15 x 737-900, 4 x 757-200, 26 x 767-400ER, 14 x 777-200ER
Continental Express: 30 x ATR42-300, 8 x ATR42-500, 3 x ATR72-210, 25 x Beech 1900D, 32 x Embraer EMB-120RT Brasilia, 31 x ERJ-145. On order: 25 x Embraer ERJ-135, 44 x ERJ-145
Colour Scheme: Continental's present livery was unveiled in February 1991. The scheme is based on blue, white and gold, with the blue tail fin the dominant feature incorporating a stylised three-dimensional globe in white latitudes and gold longitudes. A thin gold pinstripe divides the upper white fuselage from the grey belly. Simple blue 'Continental' titles are carried on the forward cabin roof.
Illustrated:
Boeing 757-200

Continental Airlines

58

CROATIA AIRLINES (OU/CTN)

Founded/First Service: 1989 as Zagreb Airlines, adopted present name in 1990
Base: Zagreb Pleso Airport, Zagreb, Croatia
Services: National airline operating international scheduled passenger and cargo services from Zagreb to Amsterdam, Berlin, Copenhagen, Düsseldorf, Frankfurt, Istanbul, London, Madrid, Manchester, Moscow, Mostar, Munich, Paris, Prague, Rome, Sarajevo, Skopje, Tel Aviv, Vienna and Zürich. Domestic flights link Zagreb with Brac, Dubrovnik, Osijek, Pula, Split and Zadar. Additional summer schedules and charters are also flown in support of the local tourist industry.
Fleet: 2 x Airbus A319, 1 x Airbus A320, 3 x ATR42-300, 4 x Boeing 737-200 Advanced, 1 x Cessna 310R, 1 x Cessna 150.
On order: 3 x Airbus A319, 1 x A320
Colour Scheme: Croatia Airlines' livery is built around the traditional red and white chequered shield of the national flag. It appears on the lower part of the tail fin in the form of an arrow flying above a light blue field, extending to the base of the fin and along the full length of the fuselage underside. The only other display on a clean white aircraft are 'CROATIA AIRLINES', or simply 'CROATIA', titles in blue, the initial letter being speeded along by a smaller red/white chequered arrow.
Illustrated: Airbus A319

CROSSAIR (LX/CRX)

Founded/First Service: 14 February 1975 as Business Flyers Basel, adopted present title 14 November 1978/2 July 1979

Base: EuroAirport Basel-Mulhouse-Freiburg, Basel, Switzerland

Services: Subsidiary of Swissair and one of Europe's foremost regional airlines, operating scheduled passenger and cargo services to 82 destinations in 28 countries from its main Basel hub and from Berne, Geneva, Lugano, Sion and Zürich. Some schedules are flown for Swissair and Lufthansa. Crossair also provides short-haul holiday charters to resorts around the Mediterranean and the Canary Islands. Associated Europe Continental Airways, trading as Crossair Europe, flies scheduled services from Basel to Marseille, Milan and Venice.

Subsidiaries and Associates: Crossair Europe (40%)

Fleet: 4 x British Aerospace (Avro) RJ85, 14 x RJ100, 1 x Boeing (McDonnell Douglas) MD-82, 11 x MD-83, 14 x Saab 340B, 32 x Saab 2000

On order: 2 x British Aerospace (Avro) RJ100, 2 x Saab 2000

Colour Scheme: Crossair's trademark, introduced in April 1993, consists of two painted patches, one on top of the other. The red Swiss rhomboid in the foreground is identical to that of the parent company, while the blue area with an irregular outline behind represents Europe, emphasised by the stars of the European Union. Along the side of the all-white fuselage is a series of ingenious graphics, stretching from nose to tail. Two small patches of red and blue develop in phases towards the rear into a complete logo, denoting Switzerland's slow progress towards entry into the EU, which Crossair hopes will eventually be achieved.

The scheme conveys Crossair's closeness to Switzerland, while at the same time illustrating its independence and commitment to Europe.

Illustrated: Saab 340B

CSA CZECH AIRLINES (OK/CSA)

Founded/First Service: 19 July 1923/28 October 1923
Base: Ruzyne Airport, Prague, Czech Republic
Services: National flag-carrier providing services to 59 international destinations, including extensive intra-European flights together with long-haul services to the Middle and Far East, and to North America. Long-haul routes link Prague with Abu Dhabi, Bangkok, Beirut, Dubai, Kuwait, Montreal, New York, Tel Aviv and Toronto. Partnership with Continental Airlines connects Prague to a further 25 cities in the United States. The domestic network incorporates Prague, Brno, Ostrava and Karlovy Vary, and there are also services to neighbouring Bratislava, Kosice, Tatry and Presov in Slovakia. Regional Air Ostrava serves some of the thinner routes as a CSA Partner airline.
Fleet: 2 x Airbus A310-300, 2 x ATR42-400, 4 x ATR72-200, 4 x Boeing 737-400, 9 x 737-500, 4 x Tupolev Tu-154M (charters only)
Colour Scheme: The fresh white overall paint scheme is complemented by the red and blue colours, which make up the national flag. Pencil-thin red and blue cheatlines run between large red 'CSA' initials (standing for the Czech title of Ceské Aerolinie) and blue 'Czechoslovak Airlines' lettering.
Illustrated: Airbus A310-300

CYPRUS AIRWAYS (CY/CYP)

Founded/First Service: 24 September 1947/6 October 1947
Base: Larnaca International Airport, Larnaca, Cyprus
Services: National flag-carrier operating scheduled international passenger services within Europe, and the Middle East and Gulf, linking Larnaca with Amman, Amsterdam, Athens, Bahrain, Beirut, Berlin, Birmingham, Brussels, Cairo, Damascus, Dresden, Dubai, Frankfurt, Hamburg, Jeddah, London Heathrow, London Gatwick, London Stansted, Manchester, Milan, Moscow, Paris, Riyadh, Rome, Salzburg, Tel Aviv, Thessaloniki, Vienna and Zürich. Some destinations are also served from Paphos. Charter flights are operated through subsidiary, Eurocypria Airlines.
Fleet: 4 x Airbus A310-200, 8 x A320-200 (three leased to Eurocypria)
Colour Scheme: The present livery introduced in late 1990 features twin 'straight through' cheatlines of royal blue and sunshine yellow below window level, separating the upper white from the lower grey fuselage. 'CYPRUS AIRWAYS' titles are promoted in blue on the mid-cabin roof. The tail fin displays the airline's white winged mountain goat (mouflon) symbol on a royal blue field, topped by two yellow bars and one blue.
Illustrated: Airbus A310-200.

DEBONAIR (2G/DEB)

Founded/First Service: 1 October 1995/19 June 1996
Base: London Luton Airport, Luton, Bedfordshire, United Kingdom
Services: An expanding low-fare airline providing scheduled passenger services from Luton to Barcelona, Düsseldorf Express, Madrid, Munich, Nice, Paris Express (Cergy-Pontoise) and Rome Ciampino, and from London Gatwick to Barcelona, where Debonair also codeshares with AB Airlines to Berlin, Lisbon, Nice and Shannon. It also links Munich with Düsseldorf and Barcelona, and flies for Air France between Paris CDG and Brussels, and between Paris and Brest and Biarritz. Services from Munich on behalf of Lufthansa, from Zürich for Swissair, and regular flights between Rome and Lourdes for the Sanctuary of Lourdes, will commence in spring 1999.
Fleet: 1 x Boeing 737-300, 10 x British Aerospace 146-200A
Colour Scheme: The new corporate colours of dark blue and magenta are prominently displayed on the gleaming all-white aircraft. The 'D', whose shapes and colours are reminiscent of the Hawaiian flowers that featured in the owner's previous airline venture in Hawaii, takes up a large part of the tail fin and adds colour to the engine cowlings. The 'D' is now superimposed on a white disk on the blue tail fin, with the blue extending downwards to wrap around the rear fuselage. The name 'debonair' is emblazoned in light and bold blue lettering across the mid-fuselage windows above a speed line, to indicate the airline's high service standards within its low-fare policy.
Illustrated: Boeing 737-300

DELTA AIR LINES (DL/DAL)

Founded/First Service: 1924 as Huff Daland Dusters, became Delta Air Service in 1928/17 June 1929. Present title adopted in 1945

Base: Hartsfield Atlanta International Airport, Atlanta, Georgia, United States

Services: World's sixth-largest airline, operating a vast domestic passenger network from seven main hubs at Atlanta, Cincinnati, Dallas/Fort Worth, Los Angeles, New York, Orlando and Salt Lake City, together with international services to Canada, the Caribbean, Central and South America, Europe and the Far East. The network encompasses over 200 destinations, and is further enhanced with an extensive domestic feeder network flown by four non-owned regional airlines operating under the *Delta Connection* banner. Low-fare services are flown by subsidiary *Delta Express*, linking northeast and Midwest points with several Florida destinations, while *Delta Shuttle* provides high-frequency services between New York, Boston and Washington DC. Delta is part of the Swissair-led *Qualiflyer* alliance.

Subsidiaries and Associates: Delta Express (100%), Delta Shuttle (100%). *Delta Connection*: Atlantic Southeast Airlines (ASA), Business Express (BEX), Comair and SkyWest Airlines

Fleet: 136 x Boeing 727-200 Advanced, 54 x 737-200 Advanced, 19 x 737-300, 2 x 737-800, 95 x 757-200, 15 x 767-200, 26 x 767-300, 43 x 767-300ER, 15 x Boeing (McDonnell Douglas) MD-11, 120 x MD-88, 16 x MD-90-30, 18 x Lockheed L-1011-1 TriStar, 6 x L-1011-250 TriStar, 15 x L-1011-500 TriStar.

On order: 67 x Boeing 737-800, 8 x 757-200, 7 x 767-300ER, 21 x 767-400ER, 12 x 777-200ER

Colour Scheme: Delta unveiled its new aircraft livery, designed by Landor Associates, in April 1997. Retaining the traditional colours of red, white and blue, brightened to make it more visible, the livery focuses on a bold, dark blue stripe that sweeps along the aircraft fuselage and reinforces the image of speed and powerful forward motion. The theme is emphasised by the highlights of red on the nose, tail and engine cowlings. On the largely blue tail fin, the 'Delta' name is reversed out in white. 'Delta Air Lines' titles sit above the windows, fronted by the blue and red Delta 'widget'. The airline's name uses a classic serif type with upper and lower case lettering to emphasise Delta's focus on friendly, personal service, which is the core of Delta's identity.

Illustrated: Boeing 767-300ER

EASYJET (U2/EZY)

Founded/First Service: 18 October 1995/10 November 1995
Bases: London Luton and Liverpool airports, United Kingdom
Services: Colourful low-fare, no-frills airline operating a scheduled UK and European network out of Luton and Liverpool. Flights from Luton serve Aberdeen, Belfast, Edinburgh, Glasgow and Inverness in the UK, and Amsterdam, Athens, Barcelona, Geneva, Madrid, Nice, Palma de Mallorca and Zürich on the Continent. The Liverpool schedule operates to Amsterdam, Barcelona, Geneva and Nice, with Belfast and Malaga to be added in spring 1999. There is also a direct Amsterdam-Nice connection. New bases may be established at Amsterdam and Athens. The airline operates a ticketless travel concept.
Fleet: 11 x Boeing 737-300.
On order: 7 x Boeing 737-300, 15 x 737-700
Colour Scheme: If you see an aircraft painted with a telephone and the telephone number 0990 29 29 29 in large orange numbers, it can only be easyJet. The telephone number, underlined in orange and spread along virtually the whole length of the fuselage above the windows, is the direct number for booking a seat. The tail fin and engine cowlings are also rendered in orange on a largely white aircraft, with the 'easyJet' titles reversed out in white.
Illustrated: Boeing 737-300

easyJet

EGYPTAIR (MS/MSR)

Founded/First Service: 7 June 1932/July 1933 as Misrair, present name adopted 10 October 1974
Base: Cairo International Airport, Heliopolis, Cairo, Egypt
Services: National flag-carrier operating passenger and cargo services throughout the Middle East and to the Far East, Africa, the United States and Europe. Cities on the European network include Amsterdam, Athens, Barcelona, Basel, Berlin, Brussels, Budapest, Copenhagen, Düsseldorf, Frankfurt, Geneva, Helsinki, Istanbul, Kiev, Larnaca, London, Madrid, Milan, Moscow, Munich, Paris CDG and Orly, Rome, Stockholm, Vienna and Zürich. Transatlantic flights link Cairo to New York and Los Angeles, while Bangkok, Osaka, Singapore, Sydney and Tokyo are reached in the Far East. Domestic flights serve Abu Simbel, Al Arish, Alexandria, Aswan, Hurghada, Luxor, Sharm-el-Sheikh and New Valley. Charters and tourist flights are also undertaken by associates Shorouk Air, owned jointly with Kuwait Airways, and Air Sinai.
Subsidiaries and Associates: Air Sinai (100%), Shorouk Air (50%)
Fleet: 2 x Airbus A300B4-200F, 9 x A300-600R, 7 x A320-200, 4 x A321-200, 3 x A340-200, 1 x Boeing 707-300C, 2 x 737-200 Advanced, 5 x 737-500, 2 x 747-300, 3 x 767-200, 2 x 767-300ER, 3 x 777-200.
On order: 2 x Airbus A340-600
Colour Scheme: EgyptAir began modernising its corporate identity in early 1996. Retaining its ancient symbol of Horus, the falcon-headed solar god of Egyptian mythology, this is now depicted in a royal blue tail fin in red and gold, and repeated on the similarly painted engine cowlings. 'EgyptAir' titles in blue forward are followed by Arabic script in red. The aircraft are otherwise painted in fresh white.
Illustrated: Airbus A340-200

EL AL ISRAEL AIRLINES (LY/ELY)

Founded/First Service: 15 November 1948/August 1949
Base: Ben Gurion International Airport, Tel Aviv, Israel
Services: National airline providing scheduled passenger and cargo services dominated by European connections and extending to the United States, Canada, Africa and the Far East. In addition to some cities served in Europe and the Middle East, long-haul routes link the capital Tel Aviv to Baltimore/Washington, Bangkok, Beijing, Boston, Chicago O'Hare, Delhi, Hong Kong, Johannesburg, Los Angeles, Miami, Montreal, Mumbai (Bombay), Nairobi, New York JFK and Newark, Tokyo and Toronto. Subsidiary Sun D'Or International operates regular, *ad hoc* and seasonal charter flights with aircraft leased from the parent company as and when required.
Subsidiaries and Associates: Sun D'Or International Airlines (100%), North American Airlines (24.9%)
Fleet: 2 x Boeing 737-200 Advanced, 1 x 747-100(SCD), 4 x 747-200B, 3 x 747-200 Combi, 2 x 747-200F, 3 x 747-400, 3 x 757-200, 4 x 757-200ER, 2 x 767-200, 2 x 767-200ER
On order: 3 x Boeing 737-700, 2 x 737-800, 1 x 747-400
Colour Scheme: The Israeli flag-carrier is introducing an updated corporate image in readiness for privatisation. The predominantly white aircraft is wrapped in a dark blue and grey ribbon, which starts on the underside of the forward fuselage and is draped over the rear roof, to end at the base and the top of the tail fin. In between the blue bands on the tail, the six-pointed Star of David provides instant recognition. Prominent blue 'EL AL' titling on the forward fuselage roof is interspersed with the Hebrew equivalent in a lighter shade, preceded by the national flag. Beneath the windows are the words 'Israel Airlines', again in English and Hebrew.
Illustrated: Boeing 737-700

EMIRATES (EK/UAE)

Founded/First Service: May 1985/25 October 1985
Base: Dubai International Airport, Dubai, United Arab Emirates
Services: Dubai flag-carrier operating scheduled passenger and cargo flights to 45 destinations throughout the Middle East and to Europe, Asia, Africa, the Indian Ocean, Australia and the Commonwealth of Independent States (CIS). Destinations served from Dubai are Abu Dhabi, Amman, Athens, Bangkok, Baku, Beirut, Cairo, Colombo, Comores, Damascus, Dar-es-Salaam, Delhi, Dhaka, Dhahran, Doha, Frankfurt, Hong Kong, Istanbul, Jakarta, Jeddah, Johannesburg, Karachi, Kuala Lumpur, Kuwait, Larnaca, London Heathrow, London Gatwick, Malé, Malta, Manchester, Manila, Melbourne, Mumbai (Bombay), Muscat, Nairobi, Nice, Paris, Peshawar, Riyadh, Rome, Singapore, Tehran, Sana'a and Zürich.
Subsidiaries and Associates: AirLanka (26%)
Fleet: 6 x Airbus A300-600R, 9 x A310-300, 9 x Boeing 777-200. On order: 17 x Airbus A330-200, 6 x A340-500, 2 x Boeing 777-300
Colour Scheme: A vast representation of the red, white, black and green United Arab Emirates flag flies upwards from the rear fuselage to cover most of the tail, providing the only flash of patriotic colours on the overall white fuselage. Gold 'Emirates' roof titles are displayed in English and Arabic, with the latter also appearing on the engine cowlings.
Illustrated: Boeing 777-200

ESTONIAN AIR (OV/ELL)

Founded/First Service: 1 December 1991
Base: Tallinn-Ylemiste Airport, Tallinn, Estonia
Services: National flag services from the capital Tallinn to Amsterdam, Copenhagen, Frankfurt, Hamburg, Helsinki, Kiev, London Gatwick, Minsk, Moscow, Oslo, Riga, Stockholm and Vilnius. No domestic services. Estonian Air became the second Baltic airline to complete its part privatisation, with Danish airline Maersk Air acquiring a 49% stake in September 1996. Another 17% is held by local investment group Baltic Cresco, with the remainder in government hands.
Fleet: 3 x Boeing 737-500, 2 x Fokker 50
Colour Scheme: Estonian Air uses the national colours of blue, black and white to good effect, although the black has been replaced by a deep shade of blue. Unusually, the upper part of the aircraft is in two-tone blue with the darker shade atop, while the lower half from below the window line is finished in white. The light blue and white tail fin, divided by the company's stylised bird/arrow motif in dark blue, is an imaginative representation of the national flag. The engine cowlings are finished in dark blue and white, with a light blue inset star. 'ESTONIAN AIR' titles below the forward windows are preceded by the airline symbol, both drawn in dark blue.
Illustrated: Boeing 737-500. *Salzburg Airport*

ETHIOPIAN AIRLINES (ET/ETH)

Founded/First Service: 26 December 1945/8 April 1946
Base: Bole International Airport, Addis Ababa, Ethiopia
Services: National carrier and one of Africa's main airlines operating flag services from Addis Ababa to points throughout Africa and to Abu Dhabi, Aden, Athens, Bangkok, Beijing, Delhi, Dubai, Frankfurt, Jeddah, Karachi, Kuwait, London Heathrow, Moscow, Mumbai (Bombay), Muscat, New York Newark, Riyadh, Rome, Sana'a and Washington. Destinations across the African continent include Abidjan, Accra, Bujumbura, Bamako, Cairo, Dar-es-Salaam, Entebbe/Kampala, Harare, Johannesburg, Kigali, Kilimanjaro, Kinshasa, Lagos, Luanda, and Nairobi. Also serves a vital domestic network incorporating more than 40 destinations.
Fleet: 1 x ATR42-300, 1 x Boeing 707-320C, 1 x 737-200, 4 x 757-200, 1 x 757-200PF, 2 x 767-200ER, 1 x 767-300ER, 1 x de Havilland Canada DHC-5A Buffalo, 4 x DHC-6 Twin Otter 300, 5 x Fokker 50, 2 x Lockheed L-100-30 Hercules
Colour Scheme: The livery is dominated by three attractive tail feathers in the national colours of green, yellow and red. These are complemented by a similarly-coloured intricate cheat line, which begins with a bright red lightning bolt at the cockpit windows and ends in a ribbon effect under the horizontal tailplane. The rampant lion of the days of the Emperor has been retained on the forward fuselage. Red 'ETHIOPIAN' lettering is displayed in English and Amharic, the official local language.
Illustrated: Fokker 50

EUROWINGS (EW/EWG)

Founded/First Service: 1 January 1993 from merger of NFD Luftverkehrs AG and RFG Regionalflug
Bases: Nuremberg and Dortmund airports, Germany
Services: Germany's largest independent regional airline providing scheduled passenger and cargo services within Germany and to neighbouring countries. Cities served are Amsterdam, Belfast, Berlin, Brussels, Cologne/Bonn, Dortmund, Dresden, Düsseldorf, Frankfurt, Guernsey, Hamburg, Hannover, Hof, Krakow, Leipzig/Halle, London, Milan, Munich, Münster/Osnabrück, Newcastle, Nuremberg, Olbia, Paderborn/Lippstadt, Palma de Mallorca, Paris, Poznan, Rome, Ronne, Saarbrücken, Stuttgart, Venice, Westerland/Sylt, Wroclaw and Zürich. Some services are flown in conjunction with Air France and KLM. Eurowings also has a busy summer and winter charter programme serving the Mediterranean area and the Canary Islands.
Fleet: 3 x Airbus A319, 12 x ATR42-300, 5 x ATR42-500, 6 x ATR72-200, 4 x ATR72-210, 6 x British Aerospace 146-200, 4 x 146-300.
On order: 1 x Airbus A319
Colour Scheme: Two speedwing arrows in red and blue, the latter with a curved contrail, form the principal element of the design, being applied on the white tail fin, engines and forward fuselage. Black 'eurowings' titling is applied on the forward upper fuselage. A blue cheat line, underscored by a thin pencil line in red, separates the white upper body from the grey underside of the aircraft. Small 'eurowings' titles break the blue cheat line at the rear, while the red pencil line is cut by the contrail of the logo.
Illustrated: Airbus A319

EVA AIR (BR/EVA)

Founded/First Service: March 1989/1 July 1991
Base: Chiang Kai-Shek International Airport, Taipei, Taiwan
Services: Privately-owned international airline serving an expanding global network of major destinations in Asia, Europe, the United States and Central America, as well as Australia and New Zealand. Cities served are Amsterdam, Anchorage, Auckland, Bangkok, Brisbane, Denpasar (Bali), Dubai, Fukuoka, Ho Chi Minh City, Hong Kong, Honolulu, Jakarta, Kuala Lumpur, London Gatwick, Los Angeles, Macau, Maldives, Manila, Melbourne, New York JFK, Osaka, Panama City, Paris, Penang, Phuket, San Francisco, Seattle, Seoul, Singapore, Surabaya, Sydney and Vienna. Dedicated all-cargo services are operated to Amsterdam, Brussels, Dallas/Fort Worth, Dubai, Jakarta, Kuala Lumpur, London, Manila, Penang and Singapore. A domestic passenger network is flown by subsidiary UNI Air, which is to be created from a merger of UNI Air, Great China Airlines and Taiwan Airlines.
Subsidiaries and Associates: Great China Airlines (25%), Taiwan Airlines (40%), UNI Air (51%)
Fleet: 5 x Boeing 747-400, 10 x 747-400 Combi, 4 x 767-200, 4 x 767-300ER, 3 x Boeing (McDonnell Douglas) MD-11, 7 x MD-11F, 2 x MD-90
On order: 2 x Boeing (McDonnell Douglas) MD-11F. LoI (letter of intent) for 6 x Airbus A340-500
Colour Scheme: The visual focal point of the airline's corporate identity is the tail fin, which features a light green globe, displayed against a dark green background. The globe is positioned so that the upper left-hand corner is cut off at an angle, said to represent the new vistas of service innovation. The vital dynamism is further enhanced by the addition of a vertical strip of orange at the fin's outer edge, imparting a sense of hi-tech innovation. Dark green, the colour of durability, creates an image of stability and reliability. The words 'EVA AIR' are applied in both greens on the forward, all-white fuselage, under a thin orange line which stretches back all the way to the fin.
Illustrated: Boeing 747-400

FEDEX (FEDERAL EXPRESS) (FM/FDX)

Founded/First Service: 1972/17 April 1973
Base: Memphis International Airport, Memphis, Tennessee, United States
Services: World's largest air freight company providing scheduled air cargo and express freight delivery services now covering 325 airports in more than 200 countries across the globe, from a superhub at Memphis, regional hubs at Newark, Oakland and Fort Worth, metroplexes at Chicago and Los Angeles, and the Anchorage gateway. Major overseas facilities are operated at London Stansted, Frankfurt, Paris, Subic Bay in the Philippines, and in Japan. The domestic network is supplemented by a number of contract carriers operating small freighters.
Fleet: 31 x Airbus A300-600F, 36 x A310-200F, 63 x Boeing 727-100F, 95 x 727-200F Advanced, 5 x 747-200F, 32 x Boeing (McDonnell Douglas) MD-11F, 10 x Cessna 208A Caravan I, 254 x 208B Caravan I Super Cargomaster, 24 x Fokker F27-500 Friendship, 8 x F27-600, 45 x McDonnell Douglas DC-10-10F, 22 x DC-10-30F
On order: 3 x Boeing (McDonnell Douglas) MD-11F
Colour Scheme: Designed by Landor Associates, the 'FedEx' brand name embraces speed, reliability, innovative technology and customer service. It is characterised by a bold sans serif typeface in dynamic shades of the purple and orange Federal Express colours, applied in large letters on the forward clean white fuselage, and in smaller size on the all-purple tail fin and rear fuselage, and on the white engine cowlings. Embedded within the primary design is an arrow, symbolising the company's speed and efficiency.
Illustrated: Airbus A300-600F

FINNAIR (AY/FIN)

Founded/First Service: 1 November 1923/20 March 1924. Originally known as Aero Oy, present name officially adopted in 1968, but used since 1953

Base: Helsinki-Vantaa Airport, Helsinki, Finland

Services: Finnish flag-carrier serving 50 international destinations. Long-haul routes are flown to Miami, New York, San Francisco and Toronto in North America and to Bangkok, Beijing, Osaka, Singapore and Tokyo in the Far East, in addition to a dense European network which serves most capital and major cities. Finnair also flies to 21 towns and cities within Finland, on a network which is one of the densest in the world in relation to population. In addition to regular scheduled traffic, Finnair also operates leisure flights to more than 60 resorts in the Mediterranean, the Canary Islands, Southeast Asia and the Caribbean.

Fleet: 6 x ATR72-200, 4 x Boeing 757-200, 4 x Boeing (McDonnell Douglas) MD-11, 10 x MD-82, 12 x MD-83, 3 x MD-87, 12 x McDonnell Douglas DC-9-51, 5 x Saab 340A, 1 x 340B 5 x Airbus A319, 3 x A320-200, 4 x A321-200

Colour Scheme: The aircraft livery is a patriotic portrayal of the national colours of white and blue, symbolising snow and sky, and comprises a blue windowline which runs the full length of the fuselage, and a tail painted to represent the Finnish flag. Attention is drawn to the blue 'FINNAIR' titles with a smart sash in three shades of blue. A small company emblem, the flying 'F', is applied on the nose in white on a blue disk. The scheme on the Boeing 757 only, has an all-white fuselage and the Finnair symbol set into a white disk on a graduated two-tone blue fin.

Illustrated: Boeing 757-200

FLYING COLOURS AIRLINES (MT/FCL)

Founded/First Service: 1996/6 March 1997
Base: Manchester airport, Manchester, United Kingdom
Services: Holiday charters flights from Manchester, London Gatwick, Glasgow, Newcastle, Bristol and Cardiff. Principal holiday destinations are Spain and the Canary Islands, with the remaining business coming from Greece, Italy, Malta, Portugal, Cyprus and Turkey. Future plans include the introduction of long-haul flights.
Fleet: 7 x Airbus A320-200, 2 x A321-200, 11 x Boeing 757-200
Colour Scheme: The airline's aircraft carry the blue, red and yellow group colours, which are represented in the form of three flags, fluttering gently in the summer breeze. This symbol is applied on the tail fin, engine cowlings and between the blue 'FLYING COLOURS' titles on the forward cabin roof. The three colours are also applied in the form of cheat lines under the windows, starting behind the crew door. The aircraft are otherwise finished in all-white.
Illustrated: Boeing 757-200

GARUDA INDONESIA (GA/GIA)

Founded: 31 March 1950, initially trading as Garuda Indonesian Airways
Base: Soekarna-Hatta International Airport, Jakarta, Indonesia
Services: National flag-carrier providing international scheduled passenger and cargo services to many regional destinations, together with long-haul flights to the Middle East, Europe and the United States. Points on the network include Adelaide, Amsterdam, Auckland, Bangkok, Brisbane, Cairns, Darwin, Dhahran, Frankfurt, Fukuoka, Hong Kong, Honolulu, Jeddah, Kuala Lumpur, London Gatwick, Los Angeles, Manila, Melbourne, Nagoya, Paris, Perth, Osaka, Riyadh, Rome, Seoul, Singapore, Sydney, Taipei, Tokyo and Zürich. Also operates an extensive domestic network linking Jakarta and 30 other points throughout the Indonesian archipelago, further expanded through the operations of subsidiary Merpati Nusantara.
Subsidiaries and Associates: Merpati Nusantara Airlines (100%)
Fleet: 8 x Airbus A300B4-200, 6 x A330-300, 1 x Boeing 737-200C, 8 x 737-300, 3 x 747-400, 7 x 737-400, 4 x 737-500, 6 x 747-200B, 3 x Boeing (McDonnell Douglas) MD-11, 3 x MD-11ER, 3 x Fokker F28-3000 Fellowship, 2 x F28-4000, 5 x McDonnell Douglas DC-10-30
On order: 3 x Airbus A330-300, 9 x Boeing 737-300, 1 x 737-500, 6 x 777-200ER
Merpati Nusantara: 1 x Airbus A300C-600, 2 x A310-300, 3 x Boeing 737-200 Advanced, 8 x de Havilland Canada DHC-6 Twin Otter 300, 13 x Fokker F27-500 Friendship, 29 x F28-4000 Fellowship, 6 x Fokker 100, 2 x IPTN (CASA) 212-200 Aviocar, 14 x IPTN/CASA CN-235-10
Colour Scheme: One of the smartest airline liveries, it was designed by Landor Associates of San Francisco and unveiled in September 1985. Its centrepiece is a modern representation of the 'Garuda', the sacred bird of Hinduism, which is displayed on the deep-blue fin in progressive shades from blue to turquoise. The five wing feathers symbolise the five national ideals. The Garuda also appears alongside dark blue 'Garuda Indonesia' titling on the all-white fuselage. The national flag is painted above the first cabin windows.
Illustrated: Airbus A300B4-200

GHANA AIRWAYS (GH/GHA)

Founded/First Service: 4 July 1958/16 July 1958
Base: Kotoka International Airport, Accra, Ghana
Services: Ghanaian flag-carrier providing international passenger and cargo services to Europe and the United States, as well as regional services to West and Southern Africa. Long-haul services are flown to Düsseldorf, London, Rome and New York, and regionally from Accra to Abidjan, Bamako, Banjul, Conakry, Cotonou, Dakar, Freetown, Harare, Johannesburg, Lagos, Lomé, Monrovia and Ouagadougou.
Fleet: 2 x McDonnell Douglas DC-9-51, 2 x DC-10-30
Colour Scheme: Based on the national tricolour, the aircraft is distinguished by a broad cheatline in red, yellow and green which widens at the base of the tail. The company insignia, comprising a black star, the symbol of African freedom, and red, yellow and green wings, is carried on the white centre engine of the DC-10, surmounted by a large national flag. The pan-African colours of the flag stand for the struggles of its forefathers (red), the country's natural resources (yellow) and agriculture (green). Black 'Ghana Airways' titles are displayed on the mid-upper fuselage.
Illustrated: McDonnell Douglas DC-10-30

GULF AIR (GF/GFA)

Founded/First Service: 24 March 1950/5 July 1950
Base: Bahrain International Airport, Muharraq, Bahrain
Services: Multinational flag-carrier of Bahrain, Oman, Qatar and the United Arab Emirates, serving an intercontinental route network of 50 destinations extending from the Middle East into Europe, East Africa, the Indian subcontinent, the Far East and Australasia. In addition to many points in the Middle East, the route system includes Amsterdam, Athens, Bangkok, Cairo, Casablanca, Chennai (Madras), Colombo, Dar-es-Salaam, Delhi, Dhaka, Entebbe/Kampala, Frankfurt, Hong Kong, Istanbul, Jakarta, Jeddah, Karachi, Khartoum, Kuala Lumpur, Larnaca, London Heathrow, Manila, Melbourne, Mumbai (Bombay), Nairobi, Paris, Rome, Singapore, Sydney and Thiruvananthapuram (Trivandrum). New York is reached via codeshare flights via London Heathrow.
Subsidiaries and Associates: Gulf Helicopters Company (100%)
Fleet: 13 x Airbus A320-200, 5 x A340-300, 10 x Boeing 767-300ER.
On order: 6 x Airbus A330-200
Gulf Helicopters: 2 x Bell 206B JetRanger, 7 x Bell 212, 8 x Bell 412
Colour Scheme: The livery features the national colours of the four states of Bahrain, Qatar, Oman and the United Arab Emirates. A maroon, green and red 'chin' flash leads the all-white fuselage, above which appear English and Arabic 'GULF AIR' titles in gold lettering. Vertical maroon, green and red bands, separated by thin white stripes, also colour the top half of the tail, below which flies a golden falcon, symbolic of the Arabian peninsula.
Illustrated:
Boeing 767-300ER

IBERIA (IB/IBE)

Founded/First Service: July 1927/14 December 1927
Base: Madrid Barajas Airport, Madrid, Spain

Services: National airline providing international flag services to all major European destinations and to North, Central and South America, Africa, the Middle East and Japan, serving 98 airports in 47 countries. In addition to Europe, where the network reaches 32 cities, Iberia has a particularly strong presence in the Americas, serving Asunçion, Bogotá, Buenos Aires, Cancun, Caracas, Guatemala City, Havana, Lima, Managua, Mexico City, Miami, Montevideo, Montreal, New York, Panama City, Quito, Rio de Janeiro, San José, San Juan, San Pedro de Sula, San Salvador, Santiago de Chile, Santo Domingo and São Paulo. Access to another 19 US destinations is available through codeshare arrangements. Extensive domestic scheduled and European leisure flights are provided through a number of subsidiary companies as well as through franchise partners Air Nostrum, operating as Iberia Regional, and Air Europa.
Subsidiaries and Associates: Aviaco (99.9%), Binter Canarias (100%), Binter Mediterraneo (100%), Viva Air (99.5%), Aerolineas Argentinas (10%), Royal Air Maroc (1.3%).
Franchises: Air Europa, Iberia Regional/Air Nostrum
Fleet: 4 x Airbus A300B4-100, 2 x A300B4-200, 22 x A320-200, 8 x A340-300, 25 x Boeing 727-200 Advanced, 5 x 737-300, 4 x 747-200B, 3 x 747-200B(SCD), 1 x 747-200F, 13 x 757-200, 2 x 767-300ER, 24 x Boeing (McDonnell Douglas) MD-87, 2 x Douglas DC-8-62F, 11 x DC-9-32, 4 x McDonnell Douglas DC-10-30.
On order: 9 x Airbus A319-100, 33 x A320-200, 19 x A321-200, 6 x A340-300, 6 x Boeing 757-200.
Aviaco: 13 x Boeing (McDonnell Douglas) MD-88, 10 x Douglas DC-9-32, 4 x DC-9-34CF. Binter: 9 x ATR72-200, 4 x CASA CN-235. *Viva Air:* 9 x Boeing 737-300
Colour Scheme: A bright sunshine livery successfully combining the red and gold colours of the national flag with an allusion to the country's holiday attractions. Triple cheat lines of red, orange and gold sweep down from behind the cockpit and along the fuselage at and above the window line. White italic 'IBERIA' titles are set into the red and orange bands of the cheat line. A quartered 'IB' logo in red and gold on the white tail carries a royal crown.
Illustrated: Airbus A340-300

ICELANDAIR (FI/ICE)

Founded/First Service: 3 June 1937/4 May 1938
Bases: Reykjavik and Keflavik Airports, Iceland
Services: National flag-carrier providing international scheduled services domestically and within Europe, as well as across the North Atlantic to the United States and Canada. Destinations are Amsterdam, Baltimore/Washington, Barcelona, Boston, Cologne/Bonn, Copenhagen, Faroe Islands, Fort Lauderdale, Frankfurt, Glasgow, Halifax, Hamburg, Helsinki, London Heathrow, Luxembourg, Miami, Milan, New York JFK, Orlando, Oslo, Palma de Mallorca, Paris, Salzburg, Stockholm, Vienna and Zürich. Domestic flights link 12 points with the capital Reykjavik, namely Akureyri, Egilsstadir, Grimsey, Hornafjördur, Husavik, Isafjördur, Kopasker, Raufarhöfn, Saudarkrokur, Thorshöfn, Vestmannaeyjar and Vopnafjördur, with further smaller communities served by subsidiary Akureyri-based Flugfelag Islands.
Subsidiaries and Associates: Flugfelag Islands (Air Iceland) (100%)
Fleet: 1 x Boeing 737-300F, 4 x 737-400, 5 x 757-200ER.
On order: 1 x Boeing 757-200, 2 x 757-300
Flugfelag Islands: 2 x de Havilland Canada DHC-6 Twin Otter 300, 2 x Fairchild SA227DC Metro 23, 3 x Fokker 50, 2 x Piper PA-31-350 Navajo Chieftain
Colour Scheme: The scheme displays the traditional Icelandic colours of white and blue in a striking, yet simple, fashion. A conventional 'straight through' window line in mid-blue is trimmed by a similarly coloured pinstripe below and contrasted by black 'ICELANDAIR' lettering above. A small Icelandic flag appears on the forward fuselage. The company symbol, a stylised flowing 'F', standing for its Icelandic name Flugleidr, rides the white tail.
Illustrated: Boeing 757-200

IRANAIR (IR/IRA)

Founded: February 1962
Base: Mehrabad Airport, Tehran, Islamic Republic of Iran
Services: National flag-carrier providing scheduled passenger and cargo services within the Middle East, to Europe, the Far East and to the Asian CIS republics. International destinations are Abu Dhabi, Almaty, Amsterdam, Ashkabad, Athens, Bahrain, Baku, Beijing, Copenhagen, Damascus, Doha, Dubai, Entebbe, Frankfurt, Geneva, Hamburg, Istanbul, Jeddah, Karachi, Kuala Lumpur, Kuwait, Larnaca, London Heathrow, Madrid, Moscow, Mumbai (Bombay), Muscat, Nairobi, Paris, Rome, Sharjah, Tashkent, Tokyo and Vienna. A domestic passenger and cargo network links 20 towns and cities in Iran. Charter flights are undertaken by Iran Air Tours.
Subsidiaries and Associates: Iran Air Tours
Fleet: 5 x Airbus A300B2-200, 2 x A300-600R, 3 x Boeing 707-320C, 2 x 727-100, 4 x 727-200 Advanced, 3 x 737-200C Advanced, 1 x 747-100, 2 x 747-200B (SCD), 1 x 747-200F, 4 x 747SP, 5 x Fokker 100. *Iran Air Tours:* 9 x Tupolev Tu-154M, 3 x Yakovlev Yak-42D
Colour Scheme: IranAir's aircraft are predominantly white, giving way to a grey underside at wing level. A thin deep blue line sweeps up the leading-edge of the tail fin and flows around to fill the upper third to form a dynamic and distinctive fin design. Below flies the Homa, a mythical bird of ancient Persia, symbolising good fortune and great strength, which is the traditional symbol of Iran Air. 'IranAir' titles are carried on the forward cabin roof, ahead of the Iranian flag and small 'The Airline of the Islamic Republic' wording. The equivalent Arabic titling appears at the rear.
Illustrated: A300-600R

JAPAN AIRLINES (JAL) (JL/JAL)

Founded/First Service: 1 August 1951/25 October 1951

Bases: Tokyo Narita Airport, Tokyo, and Kansai International, Osaka, Japan

Services: Japan's major international airline providing passenger and cargo services worldwide, serving 48 cities in 30 countries. European destinations are Amsterdam, Frankfurt, Gothenburg (cargo only), Istanbul, London Heathrow, Madrid (codeshare), Moscow, Paris, Rome and Zürich. JAL also offers high-density, high-frequency domestic flights linking Tokyo with 23 major Japanese cities. Low-cost domestic business routes are flown by a new subsidiary, JAL Express (JEX), while small communities are linked into the network through J-Air. Additionally, the JAL Group includes niche carriers Japan Asia Airways (JAA), flying certain regional routes, and Japan Air Charter (JAZ), providing charter flights to Pacific destinations.

Subsidiaries and Associates: J-Air (100%), JAL Express (JEX) (100%), Japan Air Charter (JAZ) (82%), Japan Asia Airways (JAA) (90.5%), Japan TransOcean Air (51%)

Fleet: 6 x Boeing 737-400, 2 x 747-100LR, 2 x 747-100SR, 2 x 747-100SUD, 19 x 747-200B, 8 x 747-200F, 9 x 747-300, 4 x 747-300SUD, 27 x 747-400, 8 x 747-400D, 3 x 767-200, 18 x 767-300, 7 x 777-200, 2 x 777-300, 10 x Boeing (McDonnell Douglas) MD-11, 14 x McDonnell Douglas DC-10-40.

On order: 3 x Boeing 777-200, 3 x 777-300, 15 x 747-400

J-Air: 5 x British Aerospace Jetstream 31. **JAA:** 1 x Boeing 747-100, 2 x 747-200B, 1 x 747-300, 2 x 767-300. **JAZ:** 4 x McDonnell Douglas DC-10-40

Colour Scheme: JAL's corporate identity, developed by Landor Associates of San Francisco, features a fusion of the JAL letters with a red square and grey band. JAL's 'Tsuru', a stylised version of a traditional family crest using the crane, an auspicious bird in Japan, dominates the tail of the aircraft. The straight standing black 'JAL' letters are designed to express dedication and reliability. The red square symbolises the further strengthening of the JAL corporation, with the burning enthusiasm of youth and energy. The grey band indicates a sense of vibrancy and the spirited and speedy stance taken by JAL in meeting the challenges of the future.

Illustrated: Boeing 747-400

JERSEY EUROPEAN AIRWAYS (JY/JEA)

Founded/First Service: 1 November 1979
Base: Exeter Airport, Exeter, Devonshire, United Kingdom
Services: Fast-growing UK regional airline operating a domestic network including Belfast (City Airport), Birmingham, Blackpool, Bristol, Exeter, Glasgow, Guernsey, Isle of Man, Jersey, Leeds Bradford, Londonderry, London Gatwick and Stansted, Manchester, Isle of Man and Southampton, together with European flights to Cork, Dublin and Paris Charles de Gaulle. Also provides franchise services for Air France in *Air France Express* markings from London Heathrow to Lyon and Toulouse, and from Glasgow and Edinburgh to Paris Charles de Gaulle.
Fleet: 3 x British Aerospace 146-100, 7 x 146-200, 7 x 146-300, 5 x Fokker F27-500 Friendship, 3 x Shorts 360-200
Colour Scheme: The present livery, designed by Dan Ranger and introduced in late 1990, is dominated by the airline's striking symbol appearing on the forward fuselage and on the tail fin of the almost totally white aircraft. It comprises diagonal colour stripes graduating from red via orange to primrose yellow and finishing in mid-blue, the whole forming a dynamic and inspirational delta shape. 'JERSEY EUROPEAN' titles run along the lower fuselage in blue, with the initial letter in each word emboldened. The italic serif font based on Lectura suggests movement and is expanded for maximum visibility.
Illustrated: British Aerospace 146-200

KENYA AIRWAYS (KQ/KQA)

Founded/First Service: 22 January 1977/4 February 1977
Base: Jomo Kenyatta International Airport, Nairobi, and Moi International, Mombasa, Kenya
Services: Flag-carrier operating regional services within Africa, together with schedules to
Europe, the Middle East and the Indian subcontinent, from both Nairobi and Mombasa.
Destinations include Addis Ababa, Amsterdam, Cairo, Copenhagen, Dar-es-Salaam, Dubai,
Entebbe/Kampala, Frankfurt, Harare, Johannesburg, Jeddah, Karachi, Khartoum, Kigali,
Lagos, Lilongwe, London Heathrow, Lusaka, Mumbai (Bombay), Paris Orly, Rome, Seychelles,
Stockholm and Zanzibar. Long-haul connections are available at Amsterdam through its
associate, KLM, which has a 26% stake in the airline. Domestic routes serve Nairobi,
Mombasa, Eldoret, Malindi and Kisumu. Some of these are operated on its behalf with
turboprop aircraft by Eagle Aviation as African Eagle.
Subsidiaries and Associates: Eagle Aviation
Fleet: 3 x Airbus A310-300, 2 x Boeing 737-200 Advanced, 3 x 737-300.
On order: 1 x Boeing 737-300
Colour Scheme: Quadruple cheat lines in the national colours of red and green, run along the
full length of the all-white fuselage, including a full wrap-around front and rear. Black
'Kenya Airways' titles are carried on the white cabin roof, together with the Kenyan flag,
whose colours are separated by white, which stands for peace, and includes a Masai shield
and two spears symbolising the defence of freedom. Red stylised 'KA' initials are painted on
the red tail fin, enclosed within a white circle outlined in black.
Illustrated: Boeing 737-300. *David Ezra*

KLM ROYAL DUTCH AIRLINES
(KL/KLM)

Founded/First Service: 7 October 1919/17 May 1920

Base: Amsterdam Schiphol Airport, Amsterdam, The Netherlands

Services: Dutch flag-carrier with an extensive European and intercontinental network of passenger and cargo services, linking Amsterdam with a total of 163 cities in 75 countries. The total is made up of 16 cities in Africa, six in Australia, 32 in Asia, 77 in Europe, 10 in Central and South America, four in the Caribbean, and 18 in North America. The domestic and European network is further extended through its subsidiaries KLM cityhopper, KLM uk, and KLM exel, as well as other codeshare partners. KLM has a far-reaching strategic alliance with Northwest Airlines, being joined by Alitalia.

Subsidiaries and Associates: KLM cityhopper (100%), KLM uk (100%), Martinair Holland (100%), Transavia (80%), Braathens (30%), Kenya Airways (26%). Franchise: KLM exel

Fleet: 17 x Boeing 737-300, 19 x 737-400, 3 x 747-300, 8 x 747-300 Combi, 2 x 747-300F, 5 x 747-400, 14 x 747-400 Combi, 10 x 767-300ER, 10 x Boeing (McDonnell Douglas) MD-11, 2 x Fokker 100.

On order: 8 x Boeing 737-800, 4 x 737-900, 1 x 747-400

KLM cityhopper: 13 x Fokker 50, 13 x Fokker 70

Colour Scheme: A deep blue windowline is flanked by a white underside below and a light-blue cabin roof above. The 'KLM' logotype (from the Dutch name Koninklijke Luchtvaart Maatschappij), topped by a royal crown, is painted in light blue on the all-white tail fin. The logo also appears in all-white on the cabin roof and additionally in the normal blue on the winglets of the 747-400s and MD-11s. Small 'KLM Royal Dutch Airlines' titles are set forward in the lower white fuselage stripe together with the name of each aircraft.

Illustrated: Boeing 737-300

KLM UK (UK/UKA)

Founded/First Service: 16 January 1980 through merger of Air Anglia, British Island Airways, Air West and Air Wales as Air UK, adopted present title in February 1998
Base: London Stansted Airport, Stansted, Essex, United Kingdom
Services: Britain's third-largest scheduled airline with a network of domestic and European services from several UK points, as well as a strong feeder network into its parent company's Amsterdam hub from Aberdeen, Belfast, Birmingham, East Midlands, Edinburgh, Glasgow, Humberside, Leeds/Bradford, London City, London Stansted, Manchester, Newcastle, Norwich, Sheffield and Teesside. Main routes out of the London Stansted base serve Amsterdam, Brussels, Düsseldorf, Frankfurt, Milan and Paris, together with those provided by partner airline Eurowings to Nuremberg, KLM exel to Maastricht, and Braathens to Oslo and Bergen. A separate business unit, KLM uk Channel Hopper, is dedicated to services to and from the Channel Islands of Jersey and Guernsey, currently served from London Stansted, Southampton and Amsterdam.
Fleet: 5 x ATR72-200, 10 x British Aerospace 146-300, 9 x Fokker 70, 15 x Fokker 100
Colour Scheme: A deep blue windowline is flanked by a white underside below and a light-blue cabin roof above. The 'KLM' logotype (from the Dutch name Koninklijke Luchtvaart Maatschappij), topped by a royal crown, is painted in light blue on the all-white tail fin. The logo also appears in all-white on the cabin roof followed by 'uk' to denote the UK subsidiary status.
Illustrated: Fokker 100

KOREAN AIR (KE/KAL)

Founded/First Service: June 1962
Base: Kimpo International Airport, Seoul, Korea
Services: National airline providing an extensive
schedule of international passenger and cargo

KOREAN AIR

services to more than 70 destinations regionally, and in Europe, North and South America,
the Middle East, Africa, Australia and New Zealand. Intercontinental flights serve Amsterdam,
Anchorage, Atlanta, Auckland, Bahrain, Boston, Brisbane, Cairo, Chicago O'Hare,
Christchurch, Dallas/Fort Worth, Dubai, Frankfurt, Honolulu, Jeddah, London Heathrow, Los
Angeles, Madrid, Mumbai (Bombay), New York Newark, Paris, Rome, San Francisco, São
Paulo, Sydney, Toronto, Vancouver, Washington DC and Zürich. Also provides international
all-cargo services and domestic flights to Cheju, Pusan and other smaller towns.
Fleet: 2 x Airbus A300F4-200, 5 x A300-600, 24 x A300-600R, 1 x A330-200, 4 x A330-300,
4 x Boeing 747-200B, 1 x 747-200B Combi, 9 x 747-200F, 1 x 747-300, 1 x 747-300(SCD),
25 x 747-400, 2 x 747-400 Combi, 3 x 747-400F, 2 x 747SP, 3 x 777-200ER, 2 x 777-300,
2 x Boeing (McDonnell Douglas) MD-11, 3 x MD-11F, 11 x MD-82, 1 x CASA 212-100 Aviocar,
4 x Cessna 560 Citation V Ultra, 12 x Fokker 100, 1 x Gulfstream IV
On order: 2 x Airbus A330-200, 6 x A330-300, 11 x Boeing 737-800, 11 x 737-900, 4 x 747-400,
1 x 747-400F, 1 x 777-200ER, 6 x 777-300
Colour Scheme: A pale shade of sky blue colours the entire upper fuselage and tail unit,
below which runs a silver cheat line, representing the sea. The company logo, known as the
'Taeguk', combines the red Yin and blue Yang symbols representing the opposing forces of
nature, in this case heaven and earth, with white added to show 'endless strength of
progress'. It is promoted on the tail fin and in place of the letter 'O' in the 'KOREAN AIR'
fuselage titling. This striking livery was introduced in 1984.
Illustrated: Boeing 747-400

KUWAIT AIRWAYS (KU/KAC)

Founded/First Service: March 1954/April 1954
Base: Kuwait International Airport, Safat, Kuwait
Services: National carrier operating scheduled passenger and cargo services predominantly throughout the Middle East and to Europe, with some services extending to the Far East and the United States. Destinations include Abu Dhabi, Alexandria, Amman, Amsterdam, Athens, Bahrain, Bangkok, Beirut, Cairo, Casablanca, Chicago, Colombo, Copenhagen, Damascus, Delhi, Dhahran, Dhaka, Doha, Dubai, Frankfurt, Geneva, Istanbul, Jakarta, Jeddah, Karachi, Lahore, Larnaca, London Heathrow, Luxor, Madrid, Manila, Mumbai (Bombay), Munich, Muscat, New York JFK, Paris, Riyadh, Rome, Singapore, Tehran, Thiruvananthapuram (Trivandrum) and Zürich.
Fleet: 5 x Airbus A300-600R, 1 x A300C-600, 3 x A320-200, 3 x A310-300, 4 x A340-300, 2 x Boeing 747-200B Combi, 1 x 747-400 Combi, 2 x 777-200ER, 3 x Gulfstream IV
Colour Scheme: A broad window line and tail band in ocean blue, trimmed on both sides in black and underscored by a darker blue line, provides a continuous band around the clean white fuselage. The company's black bird symbol flies reversed out in white on the largely blue tail band, again trimmed in black and darker blue. 'KUWAIT AIRWAYS' titles are applied in blue on the cabin roof, in both English and Arabic, and are repeated at the base of the tail fin in English only.
Illustrated: Airbus A300-600R

LAUDA AIR (NG/LDA)

Founded/First Service: 24 May 1979
Base: Vienna International Airport, Schwechat, Austria
Services: Provides long-haul flights from Vienna to the Far East and Australia, serving Bangkok, Denpasar (Bali), Hong Kong, Ho Chi Minh City (Saigon), Phuket, Kuala Lumpur, Sydney and Melbourne, as well as to Miami in the United States via Munich. Winter schedules also serve Malé in the Maldive Islands. An extensive European network feeds into its long-haul flights, and those of part-owner Austrian Airlines. European points served are Barcelona, Geneva, Hamburg, Lisbon, London Gatwick, Madrid, Manchester, Milan, Munich, Nice, Riga, Rome, Sofia, Split, Tallinn, Temesvar, Verona, Vilnius and Wroclaw.
Fleet: 2 x Boeing 737-300, 2 x 737-400, 1 x 737-800, 5 x 767-300ER, 2 x 777-200ER, 7 x Bombardier (Canadair) CRJ-100ER, 1 x Challenger 601, 1 x Learjet 60
Colour Scheme: Lauda Air's visual identity was revised in October 1996, to provide unobtrusive elegance, optical grace and lightness. Developed by the airline's creative director Hannes Rausch, it is highlighted by a large red 'double L' motif with a discreet golden outline, which covers the fin and alludes to the Austrian national flag. The 'double L' is repeated as the first letter in similarly bright 'Lauda' roof titling. The angel motif with the words 'Service is our success' is applied in shimmering gold behind the airline name and on the tail assembly. The upper fuselage is a mellow light grey, while a gold waterline provides separation from the dark grey underside, cut off at the rear in line with the leading-edge of the tail scheme.
Illustrated: Boeing 777-200ER

LITHUANIAN AIRLINES (TE/LIL)

Founded/First Service: 21 December 1991
Base: Vilnius International Airport, Vilnius, Lithuania
Services: National carrier operating regional and international services to points in Europe and the Commonwealth of Independent States (CIS), linking the capital Vilnius with Amsterdam, Berlin, Copenhagen, Dubai, Frankfurt, Helsinki, Istanbul, Kiev, Larnaca, London Heathrow, Moscow, Paris, Rome, St Petersburg, Samara, Stockholm, Tallinn, Tashkent, Vienna and Warsaw. Subsidiary, Air Lithuania, operates from bases at Kaunas and Palanga to Billund, Budapest, Hamburg, Kristianstad, Oslo and Prague.
Subsidiaries and Associates: Air Lithuania (100%)
Fleet: 3 x Boeing 737-200 Advanced, 1 x 737-300, 1 x Lockheed L-1329 JetStar, 2 x Saab 340B, 2 x Saab 2000, 3 x Yakovlev Yak-42, 6 x Yak-42D
Air Lithuania: 1 x ATR42-300, 1 x Tupolev Tu-134A, 3 x Yakovlev Yak-40
Colour Scheme: As befits the national flag-carrier, the latest colour scheme makes full use of the national colours of red, green and yellow. Stripes of varying thickness in the three colours are painted diagonally across the white fuselage, from the underside near the front to the base of the tail fin. The effect of speed is created by three graduated yellow stripes starting at different points along the fuselage. The otherwise white tail fin retains the company motif, which represents two red letters 'L' in a red ring. Italic 'Lithuanian Airlines' titles, also in red, take up most of the forward fuselage, preceded by the national flag.
Illustrated: Boeing 737-300. *Terry Shone*

LOT POLISH AIRLINES (LO/LOT)

Founded/First Service: 1 January 1929
Base: Warsaw Okeçie Airport, Warsaw, Poland
Services: National flag-carrier operating widespread European network, with services extending to the Middle East, North Africa, Asia and North America. Destinations include Amsterdam, Athens, Bangkok, Beijing, Berlin, Brussels, Budapest, Cairo, Chicago, Copenhagen, Damascus, Dubai, Frankfurt, Hamburg, Helsinki, Istanbul, Kiev, Larnaca, London Heathrow and Gatwick, Lvov, Madrid, Manchester, Minsk, Montreal, Moscow, Munich, New York JFK and Newark, Oslo, Paris CDG, Riga, Rome, Sofia, St Petersburg, Stockholm, Tel Aviv, Toronto, Vienna, Vilnius and Zürich. Access to other markets is provided through partnerships with other airlines, such as British Airways and American. Domestic and thinner European routes are flown by subsidiary EuroLOT.
Subsidiaries and Associates: EuroLOT (100%)
Fleet: 2 x Boeing 737-300, 7 x 737-400, 6 x 737-500, 2 x 767-200ER, 3 x 767-300ER.
On order: 2 x Boeing 737-800
EuroLOT: 3 x ATR42-300, 8 x ATR72-200. On order: 2 x ATR42-300
Colour Scheme: The aircraft livery on an all-white fuselage is centred on a large blue 'LOT' fuselage logo (LOT means flight), which is followed by a solid cheat line lining up with the top of the lettering. The blue fin contains the Polish flag behind the historic flying crane insignia in a white circle, introduced with the founding of the airline in 1929. The name appears in English on the port side and in Polish (Polskie Linie Lotnicze) on the starboard side. A blue flash of colour also extends from behind the nose to the underside of the cockpit windows.
Illustrated: Boeing 737-500

LTU INTERNATIONAL
AIRWAYS (LT/LTU)

Founded/First Service: 20 October 1955/spring 1956
Base: Düsseldorf-Rhein/Ruhr Airport, Düsseldorf, Germany
Services: One of Europe's largest holiday airlines, providing scheduled European and long-haul leisure flights, supplemented by charters, operated from all main German airports. European flights serve all the principal resort areas in the Mediterranean basin and the Canary Islands, with long-haul services flown to destinations in the Middle and Far East, Africa and North and Central America. Long-haul points served are Abu Dhabi, Bangkok, Cancun, Cape Town, Chiang Mai, Ciego de Avila, Colombo, Fort Myers, Goa, Havana, Holguin, Isla Margarita, Malé, Miami, Mombasa, Montego Bay, Orlando, Phuket, Puerto Plata, Punta Cana, San José, Santo Domingo, Santa Cruz, Tampa, Varadero and Windhoek. Spanish-based LTE International operates charters from northern Europe into Spain, while feeder services and flights to the North Sea holiday island of Sylt are provided by subsidiary RAS. LTU is now owned 49.9% by the Saie Group.
Subsidiaries and Associates: LTE International (100%), RAS Fluggesellschaft (100%)
Fleet: 6 x Airbus A330-300, 14 x Boeing 757-200, 6 x 767-300ER
Colour Scheme: The corporate colour red dominates LTU's aircraft. A bright red roof extends the whole length of the aircraft fuselage and fills the tail fin, which incorporates a white 'LTU' logo. This is repeated in red on white behind the cockpit windows. A broad red cheatline separates a white window band and the natural metal finish below. Engine cowlings are painted in white.
Illustrated: Airbus A330-300. *Terry Shone*

LUFTHANSA (LH/DLH)

Founded/First Service: 6 January 1926,
re-established after the war as Luftag
6 January 1952, changed name back to
Lufthansa 6 August 1954

Base: Frankfurt Rhein Main Airport, Frankfurt, Germany
Services: National airline providing extensive worldwide system of scheduled passenger and
cargo services, linking Germany with 302 destinations in 89 countries throughout Europe,
and in Africa, Middle East, Far East, Australasia, North America, Central America and South
America. Lufthansa, together with Air Canada, SAS, Thai Airways International, United
Airlines and Varig Brazilian Airlines, has formed the *Star Alliance*, offering a far-reaching
network with over 600 destinations in 108 countries. Some domestic and thinner European
routes are flown on its behalf by a number of regional and commuter airlines, operating as
part of TEAM Lufthansa.

Subsidiaries and Associates: Lufthansa Cityline (100%), Condor Flugdienst (55%), Lufthansa Cargo (100%), Lufthansa Cargo India (40%), DHL (32.2%). *TEAM Lufthansa:* Augsburg Airways, Contact Air, Rheintalflug, Air Dolomiti

Fleet: 13 x Airbus A300-600, 8 x A310-300, 20 x A319, 33 x A320-200, 20 x A321-100, 6 x A340-200, 12 x A340-300, 43 x Boeing 737-300, 30 x 737-500, 8 x 747-200B, 7 x 747-400 Combi, 16 x 747-400.

On order: 2 x Airbus A340-300, 10 x A340-600, 6 x Boeing 747-400

Lufthansa Cargo: 11 x Boeing 747-200F, 4 x Boeing (McDonnell Douglas) MD-11F.

On order for subsidiary: 10 x Boeing (McDonnell Douglas) MD-11F.

Lufthansa CityLine: 18 x BAe (Avro) RJ85, 31 x Bombardier (Canadair) CRJ-100.

On order for subsidiary: 13 x Bombardier (Canadair) CRJ-100, 10 x CRJ-700

Colour Scheme: Centrepoint of Lufthansa's livery is the 'flying crane' symbol, which goes back to the earliest days of German aviation, when it was carried by Deutscher Aero Lloyd. It is most prominently displayed in a yellow disk within a thin blue circle on the dark blue tail, and also appears under the cockpit in blue outline. Similarly coloured 'Lufthansa' titles in Helvetica script appear on the fuselage, which is coloured white from the wing-line upwards, and light grey below.

Illustrated: Airbus A310-300. *Andy Jacobs*

Bombardier DHC-8-200 of Augsburg Airways TEAM Lufthansa.

LUXAIR (LG/LGL)

Founded/First Service: 1961/April 1962
Base: Luxembourg (Findel) Airport, Grand Duchy of Luxembourg
Services: National airline providing scheduled passenger services within Europe only, linking Luxembourg with Alicante, Athens, Barcelona, Bastia, Berlin, Copenhagen, Faro, Frankfurt, Fuerteventura, Geneva, Hamburg, Ibiza, Lanzarote, Larnaca, Las Palmas de Gran Canaria, Lisbon, London Heathrow and Stansted, Madrid, Malaga, Manchester, Milan, Munich, Naples, Nice, Oporto, Palma de Mallorca, Paris CDG, Rimini, Rome, Saarbrücken, Salzburg, Strasbourg, Tenerife, Turin, Venice and Vienna. Also operates extensive charter flights to the Mediterranean.
Subsidiaries and Associates: Luxair Commuter (99%), Cargolux (30.5%), Luxair Executive (25%)
Fleet: 2 x Boeing 737-400, 4 x 737-500, 3 x Embraer EMB-120RT Brasilia, 2 x ERJ-145, 4 x Fokker 50
On order: 5 x Embraer ERJ-145
Colour Scheme: Pale blue and white are the dominant colours of the Luxair livery, with a broad blue window line separating the upper white and lower grey fuselage, and the blue tail promoting the company emblem in white. This consists of a stylised L-shaped arrow enclosed in an outline circle. Strong black 'LUXAIR' titling in capital letters is painted on the cabin roof behind the forward passenger door. The national and European Union flags are carried on mid-fuselage. Names of princes and châteaux, together with their respective coat of arms, are carried on the nose of the aircraft.
Illustrated: Embraer EMB-120RT Brasilia. *Author*

MAERSK AIR (DM/DMA)

Founded/First Service: 1969/January 1970
Base: Copenhagen Airport, Dragoer, Denmark
Services: Denmark's biggest independent airline providing European passenger schedules from Copenhagen to Geneva, Kristiansand, London (Gatwick), Stockholm and the Faroe Islands, and from Billund to Amsterdam, Brussels, Frankfurt, London (Gatwick), Nice, Paris, Stockholm and the Faroe Islands, feeding these services at Billund from Odense and Aalborg. Domestic flights are operated over four routes, all from Copenhagen, serving Billund, Bornholm, Esbjerg and Vojens. Leasing services and charter flights for Nordic tour operators, and for companies, associations and government bodies are also undertaken. Helicopter flights from Esbjerg to the North Sea oil fields are flown under the title of Maersk Helicopters. Subsidiary Star Air operates cargo flights on behalf of United Parcel Service (UPS), while Maersk Air UK has a scheduled passenger network out of Birmingham.
Subsidiaries and Associates: Maersk Air UK (100%), Star Air (100%), Estonian Air (49%)
Fleet: 10 x Boeing 737-300, 13 x 737-500SP, 3 x 737-700, 1 x Bombardier (Canadair) CL601-3R Challenger, 3 x Eurocopter AS 332L Super Puma, 2 x AS 365N2 Dauphin II, 3 x Fokker 50.
On order: 9 x Boeing 737-700
Maersk Air UK: 4 x Boeing 737-500, 3 x Bombardier (Canadair) CRJ-200LR, 2 x British Aerospace One-Eleven-500, 1 x Jetstream 41. **On order for subsidiary:** 3 x CRJ-200LR.
Star Air: 7 x Boeing 727-100F
Colour Scheme: The aircraft livery employs an overall base colour of light blue with twin cheatlines below the windows in medium and dark blue trimmed in white. The seven-pointed star company logo is promoted in white within a white outline box, both on the tail and the forward fuselage in front of 'MAERSK' titles.
Illustrated: Boeing 737-700

MALAYSIA AIRLINES (MH/MAS)

Founded/First Service: April 1971/9 June 1971
Base: Kuala Lumpur International Airport, Sepang, Malaysia
Services: National flag-carrier operating an extensive domestic and regional network, with services extending to the South Pacific, North Asia, Africa, the Middle East, Europe and the Americas, reaching 77 destinations. Points served westward include Amman, Amsterdam, Beirut, Cairo, Cape Town, Chennai (Madras), Colombo, Delhi, Dhaka, Dubai, Frankfurt, Istanbul, Jeddah, Johannesburg, Karachi, London Heathrow, Maldives, Mauritius, Munich, Paris, Rome, Tehran, Seychelles, Zagreb and Zürich. In the Americas the airline links Kuala Lumpur to Buenos Aires, Los Angeles, New York and Vancouver. The domestic network encompasses 36 towns and cities.
Fleet: 11 x Airbus A330-300, 2 x Boeing 737-300F, 39 x 737-400, 9 x 737-500, 2 x 747-200F, 1 x 747-300(SCD), 15 x 747-400, 2 x 747-400C, 5 x 777-200ER,
2 x Boeing (McDonnell Douglas) MD-11F, 6 x de Havilland Canada DHC-6 Twin Otter 310, 10 x Fokker 50, 2 x McDonnell Douglas DC-10-30
On order: 1 x Boeing 737-700BBJ, 6 x 747-400, 7 x 777-200ER
Colour Scheme: The modern MAS livery is highlighted by the fresh white upper fuselage carrying red and mid-blue cheat lines with a trailing sweep at the rear to accentuate design symmetry and balance. The corporate image in red and blue, dividing equally at mid-spine, dominates the tail fin. It retains the essence of the Kelantan *Wau Bulan*, or Moon Dragon kite, while achieving a more aerodynamic posture. Predominantly blue 'Malaysia' titles appear on the forward cabin roof preceded by the national flag. Within the unique italicised typeface, the letters 'm', 'a' and 's' bear red clippings to denote the initials of the airline's full name.
Illustrated: Boeing 777-200

malaysia
AIRLINES

97

MALÉV HUNGARIAN AIRLINES
(MA/MAH)

Founded/First Service: 26 April 1946 as Maszovlet, present name adopted 25 November 1954
Base: Budapest Ferihegy Airport, Budapest, Hungary
Services: National airline with a predominantly intra-European and Near East network serving most capital cities and other major industrial and business centres, as well as long-haul routes to the United States, China and Thailand. Services extend from Budapest to Amsterdam, Athens, Bangkok, Barcelona, Beijing, Beirut, Berlin, Brussels, Bucharest, Cairo, Cologne/Bonn, Copenhagen, Damascus, Düsseldorf, Frankfurt, Hamburg, Helsinki, Istanbul, Kiev, Larnaca, London Heathrow, Madrid, Milan, Moscow, Munich, New York, Paris, Prague, Rome, Sofia, St Petersburg, Stockholm, Stuttgart, Tel Aviv, Thessaloniki, Tirana, Vienna, Warsaw and Zürich.
Fleet: 6 x Boeing 737-200 Advanced, 2 x 737-400, 2 x 767-200ER, 6 x Fokker 70, 5 x Tupolev Tu-154B-2
Colour Scheme: The current livery features a sweep of blue at the rear of the clean overall white fuselage and the tail, which carries fin flashes in the national colours of red, white and green, going back to the earliest days of Hungary's history. Blue 'MALEV' titles appear on the forward cabin roof, alongside the flag and additional smaller 'Hungarian Airlines' lettering. The nose cone is also painted blue.
Illustrated: Boeing 767-200ER

MARTINAIR (MP/MPH)

Founded: 24 May 1958 as Martin's Air Charter, present title adopted April 1968
Base: Amsterdam Schiphol Airport, Amsterdam, The Netherlands
Services: KLM Royal Dutch Airlines subsidiary operating worldwide cargo charter flights, principally over the Europe-Far East 'corridor' via the Middle East, and to Australia, Africa, Mexico, South America and the United States. Also provides passenger inclusive-tour services from Amsterdam, serving a number of resorts in Europe, Mexico, Canada and Thailand, together with scheduled services across the North Atlantic to the United States, the Dominican Republic, Jamaica, Cuba, Puerto Rico and Barbados. Executive flights are offered, and Martinair also undertakes contract flights on behalf of the Department of Public Works.
Fleet: 2 x Boeing 747-200C(SCD), 1 x 747-200F, 6 x 767-300ER, 4 x Boeing (McDonnell Douglas) MD-11CF, 2 x MD-11F, 2 x Cessna 650 Citation VI, 1 x Dornier 228-200
Colour Scheme: A warm red window line runs the full length of the fuselage, terminating at an angle just short of the horizontal tailplane. A stylised red 'M' shaped into an arrow dominates the white fin. Black 'Martinair' titles are displayed on the upper fuselage.
Illustrated: Boeing 767-300ER

MERIDIANA (IG/ISS)

Founded/First Service: 24 March 1963 as Alisarda, present name adopted September 1991
Base: Costa Smeralda Airport, Olbia, Sardinia, Italy
Services: Scheduled domestic passenger flights and cross-border services to 10 destinations in six European countries, including additional seasonal routes from Sardinia. Points on the network are Amsterdam, Barcelona, Bergamo, Bologna, Cagliari, Catania, Florence, Frankfurt, Geneva, Genoa, London (served from Florence, and seasonally, from Cagliari and Olbia), Lyon, Milan, Munich, Naples, Nice, Palermo, Paris, Pisa, Rome, Turin, Venice, Verona and Zürich.
Fleet: 1 x Bell 412, 12 x Boeing (McDonnell Douglas) MD-82, 4 x British Aerospace 146-200, 5 x McDonnell Douglas DC-9-51
Colour Scheme: The colour scheme is notable for the white circle on a predominantly warm red tail fin, incorporating the company insignia composed of meridians — imaginary lines joining the North and South Poles at right angles to the Equator. The base of the fin is supported by a thin yellow and broader purple line. A similar yellow cheatline is sandwiched between the red and purple lines extending the full length of the fuselage below the windows. Black 'Meridiana' titles appear forward ahead of the wing. The 146 carries the company symbol on the outer engines.
Illustrated: Boeing (McDonnell Douglas) MD-82

MIDDLE EAST AIRLINES — MEA
(ME/MEA)

Founded/First Service: May 1945/20 November 1945 as Middle East Airlines Air Liban, present title adopted in 1965
Base: Beirut International Airport, Beirut, Lebanon
Services: National airline operating scheduled passenger and cargo services from Beirut to destinations throughout the Middle East, North and West Africa, Europe, the Far East, Australia and South America. Points served include Abidjan, Abu Dhabi, Accra, Amman, Ankara, Athens, Bahrain, Berlin, Brussels, Bucharest, Cairo, Colombo, Copenhagen, Damascus, Dhahran, Doha, Dubai, Frankfurt, Geneva, Istanbul, Jeddah, Kano, Kuala Lumpur, Lagos, Larnaca, London Heathrow, Madrid, Nice, Paris CDG, Riyadh, Rome, São Paulo, Sydney, Tunis and Zürich. Connections to North America are provided at Paris Charles de Gaulle in association with strategic partner Air France.
Fleet: 2 x Airbus A320-200, 2 x A321-200, 3 x A310-200, 2 x A310-300, 3 x Boeing 707-320C (for sale)
Colour Scheme: MEA introduced a modernised livery in 1996, to coincide with its fleet renewal programme. Its all-white aircraft now carry 'MEA' initials in red, green and turquoise on the lower forward fuselage. The airline name is repeated in full and in the same colours under the rear windows in English, and in Arabic above, but in green throughout. The tail fin is dominated by a green Cedar of Lebanon, mentioned in the Bible, which symbolises strength, holiness and eternity, while the red and white, taken from the national flag, stands for self-sacrifice and peace. The cedar is also featured on the engine cowlings.
Illustrated: Airbus A320-200

MONARCH AIRLINES (OM/MON)

Founded/First Service: 1 June 1967/5 April 1968
Base: London Luton Airport, Luton, Bedfordshire, United Kingdom
Services: A major UK holiday airline providing extensive charter flights and inclusive tour packages for leading tour operators, including sister company Cosmos, from Luton, London Gatwick, London Stansted, Manchester, Birmingham, Leeds Bradford and Glasgow to Europe and the Mediterranean area. Long-haul flights are also undertaken to such destinations as the United States, Bahamas, Cuba, Dominican Republic, Mexico, Brazil, Kenya, Malaysia, Sri Lanka and Thailand. Also flies scheduled 'leisure' routes since July 1986, from Luton to Alicante, Mahon, Malaga and Tenerife in the Canary Islands.
Fleet: 5 x Airbus A320-200, 3 x A321-200, 4 x A300-600R, 2 x A330-200, 7 x Boeing 757-200ER, 1 x McDonnell Douglas DC-10-30
Colour Scheme: Golden yellow and black 'straight through' cheatlines contrast sharply with the predominantly white fuselage and tail, which carries the company's crowned 'M' insignia. Bold black 'Monarch' titles appear behind the forward passenger door.
Illustrated: Boeing (McDonnell Douglas) DC-10-30. *Terry Shone*

NORTHWEST AIRLINES (NW/NWA)

Founded/First Service: 1 August 1926/1 October 1926

Base: Minneapolis St Paul International Airport, St Paul, Minnesota, USA

Services: World's fourth-largest airline operating an extensive network of scheduled passenger services throughout the Americas, and across the Atlantic to Europe and Africa, and across the Pacific to Asia and Australia. Together with affiliated airlines operating under the *Northwest Airlink* banner, the network encompasses some 240 destinations in 22 countries, and this is further extended through major strategic alliance partnerships with KLM Royal Dutch Airlines and Continental Airlines, adding up to a total of 400 destinations in 80 countries. Cities served outside the Americas include Amsterdam, Bangkok, Beijing, Delhi, Frankfurt, Fukuoka, Guam, Hong Kong, London Gatwick, Manila, Nagoya, Osaka, Paris, Saipan, Seoul, Shanghai, Singapore, Taipei and Tokyo. Main hubs are operated at Minneapolis St Paul, Detroit, Memphis and Tokyo.

Subsidiaries and Associates: *Northwest Airlink:* Express Airlines (100%), Mesaba Airlines (32.7%)

Fleet: 63 x Airbus A320-200, 40 x Boeing 727-200 Advanced, 3 x 747-100, 22 x 747-200B, 8 x 747-200F, 10 x 747-400, 48 x 757-200, 8 x Boeing (McDonnell Douglas) MD-82, 19 x McDonnell Douglas DC-9-10, 113 x DC-9-30, 12 x DC-9-41, 35 x DC-9-51, 15 x DC-10-30, 21 x DC-10-40

On order: 50 x Airbus A319-100, 7 x A320-200, 16 x A330-300, 4 x Boeing 747-400, 25 x 757-200

Northwest Airlink: 18 x British Aerospace (Avro) RJ85, 8 x British Aerospace Jetstream 31, 18 x Bombardier DHC-8-100, 43 x Saab 340A, 54 x Saab 340B.

On order for subsidiary: 18 x BAe (Avro) RJ85

Colour Scheme: The Northwest corporate signature was introduced in June 1989. It focuses on an updated rendering of Northwest's call letters in white near the top of the tail, expressing the 'N' explicitly, while the 'pointer' to its left strongly suggests the letter 'W' and a compass pointing northwest. The importance of the red tail is emphasised by extending the colour over the entire top of the fuselage above a strong presence of grey, to communicate a note of seriousness and efficiency. A deep blue tapered speedstripe underscores the grey. Large 'NORTHWEST' lettering is applied in white on grey.

Illustrated: Airbus A320-200.

OLYMPIC AIRWAYS (OA/OAL)

Founded: 1 January 1957
Base: Athens Hellenikon International Airport, Athens, Greece
Services: National airline operating scheduled passenger and cargo services from Athens and a secondary hub at Thessaloniki to most European and neighbouring Middle Eastern cities, as well as to destinations in Africa, the Far East, Australia and North America. Long-haul points on the network include Bangkok, Boston, Johannesburg, Melbourne, Montreal, Nairobi, New York JFK, Rio de Janeiro, São Paulo, Sydney and Toronto. Also serves extensive domestic route system serving 34 destinations on the mainland and the Greek islands, many flown by subsidiary, Olympic Aviation, which also undertakes charters and helicopter flights. Another subsidiary, Macedonian Airlines, provides charter flights with aircraft from the parent company.
Subsidiaries and Associates: Olympic Aviation (100%), Macedonian Airlines (100%)
Fleet: 4 x Airbus A300B4-100, 2 x A300B4-200, 2 x A300-600R, 2 x A340-300, 2 x 727-200 Advanced, 11 x 737-200 Advanced, 7 x 737-400, 4 x 747-200B
On order: 2 x Airbus A340-300, 8 x Boeing 737-800
Colour Scheme: The famous six Olympic rings are painted in their traditional colours on the dark blue tail fin, which is an extension of the narrow pencil line carried above the windows. The same dark blue window line is wrapped around the fuselage and underscored by a dark blue pencil line. Expanded 'OLYMPIC' lettering, also in dark blue, is carried on the forward half of the upper white fuselage behind a national blue and white pendant.
Illustrated: Airbus A340-600R

PAKISTAN INTERNATIONAL AIRLINES (PK/PIA)

Founded/First Service: 1954/7 June 1954
Base: Quaid-i-Azam International Airport, Karachi, Pakistan
Services: National flag-carrier operating a scheduled services network incorporating 55 international destinations in 37 countries in Africa, Europe, the Middle and Far East and North America. Long-haul flights serve Amsterdam, Athens, Beijing, Cairo, Copenhagen, Frankfurt, Istanbul, London, Manchester, Manila, Moscow, Nairobi, New York, Paris, Rome, Tokyo, Toronto, Washington and Zürich. A 37-point domestic network is also flown, centred on the main cities of Karachi, Lahore, Islamabad and Peshawar.
Fleet: 10 x Airbus A300B4-200, 6 x A310-300, 2 x Boeing 707-320C, 6 x 737-300, 6 x 747-200B, 2 x 747-200B(SCD), 2 x de Havilland Canada DHC-6 Twin Otter 300, 12 x Fokker F27-200 Friendship, 1 x F27-400
Colour Scheme: The PIA livery makes good use of the national colours of green and white, enhanced by two-tone green and light blue bands wrapped around the lower fuselage, starting just ahead of the wing. The green is continued over the whole of the underside of the aircraft to the rear of the fuselage, making for a most attractive and unusual scheme. 'Pakistan' titles in green above their Urdu equivalent are displayed on the upper forward fuselage. White 'PIA' initials highlight the all-green tail fin.
Illustrated: Airbus A310-300

QANTAS AIRWAYS (QF/QFA)

Founded: 16 November 1920
Bases: Sydney Kingsford Smith Airport, Mascot, New
South Wales, and Melbourne International, Australia
Services: Australia's main international airline
providing scheduled passenger and cargo services
from Sydney and other state capitals to 30 countries

in Asia Pacific, Europe, North America and southern Africa. Services take in Auckland, Bangkok,
Beijing, Christchurch, Denpasar (Bali), Frankfurt, Fukuoka, Harare, Ho Chi Minh City, Hong Kong,
Honiara, Honolulu, Jakarta, Johannesburg, Kuala Lumpur, London Heathrow, Los Angeles, Manila,
Mumbai (Bombay), Nagoya, Noumea, Osaka, Papeete, Port Moresby, Port Vila, Rome, Sapporo,
Seoul, Shanghai, Singapore, Taipei, Tokyo and Wellington. Qantas is a part of the '*oneworld*'
alliance headed by British Airways, which has a 25% shareholding. A domestic network is boosted
by feeder services provided by associated carriers.
Subsidiaries and Associates: Airlink (100%), Eastern Australia Airlines (100%), Southern Australia
Airlines (100%), Sunstate Airlines (100%), Australian Air Express (50%), Air Pacific (17.5%)
Fleet: 3 x Airbus A300B4-200, 15 x Boeing 737-300, 21 x 737-400, 3 x 747-200B, 2 x 747-200(SCD),
6 x 747-300, 18 x 747-400, 7 x 767-200ER, 21 x 767-300ER.
On order: 3 x Boeing 747-400
Airlink: 5 x British Aerospace 146-100, 5 x 146-200, 2 x 146-300. *Eastern Australia:* 4 x British
Aerospace Jetstream 31, 7 x Bombardier DHC-8-100. *Southern Australia:* 2 x British Aerospace 146-
200A, 3 x Bombardier DHC-8-100, 2 x Cessna 404 Titan II. *Sunstate:* 4 x Bombardier DHC-8-100,
5 x de Havilland Canada DHC-6 Twin Otter 300, 4 x Shorts 360-100, 4 x Shorts 360-300
Colour Scheme: The Qantas image is the work of Sydney design consultant Tony Lunn & Associates
and was officially unveiled in June 1984. It features an all-white fuselage with a strong tail fin
arrangement in which the warm red is extended down around the fuselage. The red fin is trimmed
in gold at the leading-edge for added elegance. The tail shape has been designed into triangular
logos for the engine cowlings. Black 'QANTAS' titles are displayed near the forward passenger door,
complemented by additional 'The Australian Airline' wording below, also in black.
Illustrated: Boeing 747-400

QATAR AIRWAYS (QR/QTR)

Founded/First Service: 20 October 1993/20 January 1994
Base: Doha International Airport, Doha, Qatar
Services: Designated the national carrier alongside Gulf Air and operating a growing network of scheduled passenger and cargo services within the Middle East, extending to the Indian subcontinent, the Far East, Africa and Europe. Destinations are Abu Dhabi, Amman, Bangkok, Beirut, Cairo, Colombo, Damascus, Dhahran, Dhaka, Doha, Jeddah, Karachi, Kathmandu, Khartoum, Kuwait, Lahore, London Heathrow, Manila, Mumbai (Bombay), Munich, Peshawar and Thiruvananthapuram (Trivandrum).
Fleet: 3 x Airbus A300-600R, 4 x Boeing 727-200 Advanced, 2 x 747SR
On order: 4 x Airbus A320-200
Colour Scheme: The attractive new livery of Qatar Airways, now the national carrier of this Gulf State, is noticeable for its unusual silver grey upper fuselage and tail fin, above a white-painted lower half from under the windows. The only other colour is the maroon of the national flag, expressed both on the 'QATAR AIRWAYS' titles in English and Arabic on the front aircraft roof, and on the tail fin, where a desert gazelle is superimposed over a gradated silver moon.
Illustrated: Airbus A300-600R. *Terry Shone*

REGIONAL AIRLINES (VM/RGI)

Founded/First Service: 1 January 1992 through merger of Air Vendée and Airlec
Base: Nantes-Atlantique Airport, Nantes, France
Services: Appropriately named regional airline providing scheduled passenger services within France, and across the border to neighbouring European countries, serving Amsterdam, Barcelona, Bilbao, Birmingham, Brussels, Copenhagen, Düsseldorf, Geneva, Lisbon, Madrid, Milan, Münster/Osnabrück, Oporto, Stuttgart and Turin. Services within France radiate from Nantes, Bordeaux, Clermont-Ferrand, Lyon, Toulouse and Rouen, also taking in Angoulême, Caen, Dijon, Le Havre, Limoges, Marseille, Montpellier, Mulhouse, Nice, Pau, Poitiers, Rennes, St Brieuc, Strasbourg and Toulon.
Fleet: 9 x British Aerospace Jetstream 31, 8 x Embraer EMB-120ER Brasilia, 6 x ERJ-145, 5 x Saab 340B, 8 x Saab 2000
On order: 5 x Embraer ERJ-135, 5 x ERJ-145
Colour Scheme: French navy and sky blue bands of different widths follow the line of the tail fin's leading-edge up, across the top and down to the base of the rear fuselage. The company's logo, representing a gull flying over a graduated sky blue globe, appears in red near the centre of the tail and below the cockpit windows, together with small 'REGIONAL Airlines' titles in navy and sky blue. A large red gull with shortened navy 'REGIONAL' are displayed across the largely white fuselage.
Illustrated: Embraer ERJ-145

ROYAL AIR MAROC (AT/RAM)

Founded: 25 June 1953
Base: Mohammed V International Airport, Casablanca, Morocco
Services: National airline providing scheduled passenger and cargo services to North and West Africa, the Middle East, and to most major European destinations, as well as across the Atlantic to New York and Montreal. Destinations served include Abidjan, Amsterdam, Athens, Barcelona, Bastia, Bordeaux, Brussels, Cairo, Conakry, Dakar, Damascus, Frankfurt, Geneva, Istanbul, Jeddah, Libreville, Lisbon, London Heathrow, Lyon, Madrid, Malabo, Malaga, Marseille, Milan, Munich, Nice, Nouakchott, Paris, Riyadh, Rome, Strasbourg, Toulouse, Tripoli, Tunis, Zürich, and the Canary Islands. Also operates domestic flights including frequent shuttles between Casablanca and Marrakech, Agadir, Ouarzazate, Tangier and Fez.
Fleet: 2 x ATR42-300, 6 x Boeing 737-200 Advanced, 7 x 737-400, 6 x 737-500, 2 x 737-800, 1 x 747-200B(SCD), 1 x 747-400, 2 x 757-200
Colour Scheme: A green, white and red windowline separates the upper white fuselage from the grey underside. It tapers at both ends and promotes strong 'royal air maroc' titles in lower case red. The centrepiece of the national flag is the green pentangle (or seal of Solomon), which adorns the tail in the form of a shooting star, whose red trail emanates from below bold red 'RAM' initials at the base.
Illustrated: Boeing 747-400

ROYAL BRUNEI AIRLINES (BI/RBA)

Founded/First Service: 18 November 1974/14 May 1975
Base: Bandar Seri Begawan Airport, Brunei Negara Darussalam
Services: National airline providing flag services to regional destinations and to the Middle East and Europe. Points served include Abu Dhabi, Balikpapan, Bangkok, Beijing, Bintulu, Brisbane, Calcutta, Darwin, Denpasar (Bali), Dubai, Frankfurt, Hong Kong, Jakarta, Jeddah, Kota Kinabalu, Kuala Lumpur, Kuching, Labuan, London Heathrow, Manila, Miri, Osaka Kansai International, Perth, Singapore, Surabaya, Taipei and Yangon. Additional destinations are accessed through a number of international alliances.
Fleet: 2 x Boeing 757-200, 9 x 767-200ER, 2 x Fokker 100
Colour Scheme: Royal Brunei's livery was adopted in early 1986 to coincide with the delivery of its first Boeing 757. It is based strongly on the colours of the national flag, where yellow represents the Sultan, and black and white his two chief ministers. The design features a yellow lower fuselage, separated from the white roof by pinstripes in yellow and black, with both colours sweeping upwards over the tail fin and painting a continuous pattern. The national arms, depicting a vertical winged support standing on the Muslim crescent, forms the main feature of the fin. Black 'Royal Brunei' titles are worn on the cabin roof alongside the national flag.
Illustrated: Boeing 767-200ER. *Terry Shone*

ROYAL JORDANIAN (RJ/RJA)

Founded/First Service:
8 December 1963/15 December 1963

Base: Queen Alia International Airport, Amman, Jordan

Services: Jordan's national flag-carrier operating an international scheduled passenger and cargo network throughout the Middle East, and to the Far East, North Africa, Europe and the United States. Destinations include Abu Dhabi, Aden, Al Ain, Amman, Amsterdam,

Ankara, Athens, Bahrain, Bangkok, Beirut, Berlin, Brussels, Bucharest, Cairo, Calcutta, Casablanca, Chicago O'Hare, Copenhagen, Damascus, Delhi, Dhahran, Doha, Dubai, Frankfurt, Geneva, Istanbul, Jakarta, Jeddah, Karachi, Kuala Lumpur, Kuwait, Larnaca, London Heathrow, Madrid, Moscow, Mumbai (Bombay), Muscat, New York JFK, Paris Orly, Riyadh, Rome, Sana'a, Tunis and Vienna. Subsidiary Royal Wings operates domestic flights between Amman and Aqaba, as well as some local flights with turboprop equipment, while Arab Wings undertakes executive flights.

Subsidiaries and Associates: Arab Wings (100%), Royal Wings (100%)

Fleet: 2 x Airbus A310-200, 4 x A310-300, 3 x A320-200, 2 x Boeing 707-320C, 5 x Lockheed L-1011-500 TriStar   *Arab Wings:* 1 x Cessna 340A, 2 x Sabreliner 75A

Royal Wings: 2 x Bombardier DHC-8-300

Colour Scheme: The present livery, created by Landor Associates of San Francisco and introduced in 1986, was designed to convey a spirit of Jordan's heritage, using majestic gold and red cheat lines along a unique charcoal grey upper fuselage. The gold crown of the Hashemite Kingdom dominates the tail fin, which also features subtle tapered speed bands in dark grey and a red tip. 'ROYAL JORDANIAN' titles in gold are applied along the cabin roof in both English and Arabic. The Jordanian flag, which incorporates a seven-pointed white star in a red field signifying the first seven verses of the Koran, is painted on the rear fuselage.

Illustrated: Airbus A320-200

ROYAL NEPAL AIRLINES (RA/RNA)

Founded: 1 July 1958
Base: Tribhuvan Airport, Kathmandu, Nepal
Services: National flag-carrier operating international scheduled flights from Kathmandu to regional destinations, together with long-haul flights to Frankfurt, London Gatwick and Paris via Dubai. Regional points within Asia and the Indian subcontinent are Bangkok, Calcutta, Delhi, Hong Kong, Mumbai (Bombay), Osaka, Shanghai and Singapore. Vital domestic services are provided to points on the southern slopes of the Himalayas and to isolated inland valleys totalling 29 destinations, including the principal towns of Biratnagar, Nepalgunj, Pokhara and Surket.
Fleet: 2 x Boeing 757-200, 1 x British Aerospace (HS) 748-2B,
8 x de Havilland Canada DHC-6 Twin Otter, 1 x Pilatus PC-6B/B1-H2 Turbo Porter
Colour Scheme: A pure white fuselage conveys the snow-capped peaks of the Himalayas, crossed by twin diagonal fin bands in the national colours of red and blue, which continue onto the rear fuselage. Blue 'Royal Nepal Airlines' titles are displayed on the forward cabin roof, in English on the left and Nepali in Devanagari script on the right-hand side, and preceded by the unique 'double triangle' national flag, the only one in the world that is not rectangular. The flag incorporates the crescent moon and the sun, signifying the hope that the country may live as long as these two astral bodies. The airline's traditional 'winged Buddha' symbol is painted beneath the cockpit windows.
Illustrated: Boeing 757-200

Royal Nepal Airlines

RYANAIR (FR/RYR)

Founded/First Service: May 1985
Base: Dublin Airport, Dublin, Ireland
Services: Scheduled low-fare passenger flights from the Irish Republic to points in the United Kingdom, serving Birmingham, Bournemouth, Bristol, Cardiff, Glasgow, Liverpool, London Gatwick, London Stansted, Luton, Manchester and Teesside. London Stansted is also linked to Kerry in the Irish Republic, and to Carcassonne, Glasgow (Prestwick), Kristianstad, Oslo (Torp), Pisa, Rimini, St Etienne, Stockholm (Skvasta) and Venice (Treviso). Charter services to European cities and resort areas are flown from both Dublin and London Stansted.
Fleet: 21 x Boeing 737-200 Advanced
On order: 25 x Boeing 737-800 (plus 20 options)
Colour Scheme: A 'flying' variation of the Irish harp, which has been a national symbol since at least the 15th century, is displayed in yellow on a mid-blue tail fin. The mid-blue belly of the aircraft is separated from an otherwise white fuselage by a broad yellow band that dips down below the cockpit. Blue 'RYANAIR' titles are carried above the window line forward of the wing, preceded by the yellow harp. Four aircraft are now painted in the liveries of various advertisers, including Jaguar, Kilkenny, Tipperary Crystal and The Sun/News of the World newspaper.
Illustrated: Boeing 737-200 Advanced. *James Lee*

SABENA WORLD AIRLINES (SN/SAB)

Founded/First Service: 23 March 1923
Base: Brussels-National Airport, Zaventem, Belgium
Services: Comprehensive European scheduled services network and still expanding strong African presence, together with long-haul flights to Newark and Montreal in North America, and to Bangkok and Phuket in Thailand, and Tokyo in Japan. Other points in the United States and South America are reached in conjunction with partner airlines, bringing the total network to 100 cities in 46 countries. African destinations include Abidjan, Bamako, Banjul, Conakry, Cotonou, Dakar, Douala, Entebbe, Johannesburg, Kigali, Kinshasa, Lagos, Lomé, Luanda, Nairobi, Ouagadougou and Yaounde. Sabena is part of the Swissair-led *Qualiflyer* alliance grouping, which also includes Austrian Airlines, AOM French Airlines, Delta Air Lines, TAP Air Portugal and Turkish Airlines.

Subsidiaries and Associates: DAT Belgian Regional Airline (99.9%), Sobelair (72.3%)
Fleet: 3 x Airbus A330-300, 1 x A330-200, 2 x A340-200, 2 x A340-300, 13 x Boeing 737-200 Advanced, 6 x 737-300, 3 x 737-400, 6 x 737-500, 2 x 747-300 (SCD), 2 x Boeing (McDonnell Douglas) MD-11, 4 x Bombardier DHC-8-300
On order: 26 x Airbus A319, 5 x A320, 3 x A321-200, 2 x A330-200
DAT: 6 x British Aerospace 146-200, 14 x BAe (Avro) RJ85, 9 x RJ100
Sobelair: 4 x Boeing 737-300, 3 x 737-400, 2 x 767-300ER
Colour Scheme: The Belgian flag-carrier introduced a new livery at the end of 1998, replacing the warmer image, which came into use from April 1993. The new corporate identity retains the traditional letter 'S', but this is now set into a white circle with blue curved dynamic lines, the whole applied on a blue tail fin. This representation is repeated on the engine cowlings. The previously understated and shadowed lettering has been replaced with larger and bolder blue 'sabena' titles, which take up most of the forward fuselage. Small Belgian and European flags are painted near the rear access door.
Illustrated: Airbus A340-200

SAUDI ARABIAN AIRLINES (SV/SVA)

Founded/First Service:
1945/4 March 1947
Base: King Abdul Aziz
International Airport,
Jeddah, Saudi Arabia

Services: National airline operating scheduled passenger and cargo services to more than 50 destinations throughout the Middle East, and to the Indian subcontinent, the Far East, Africa, Europe and the United States. A 26-point domestic network is also operated. Cities served outside the Middle East are Addis Ababa, Algiers, Athens, Bangkok, Cairo, Casablanca, Chennai (Madras), Colombo, Delhi, Dhaka, Frankfurt, Geneva, Istanbul, Islamabad, Johannesburg, Kano, Khartoum, Kuala Lumpur, Lahore, Larnaca, London Heathrow, Manila, Mumbai (Bombay), Nairobi, New York JFK, Paris CDG, Rome, Singapore, Tunis and Washington.
Fleet: 11 x Airbus A300-600, 20 x Boeing 737-200 Advanced, 7 x 747-100, 2 x 747-200F, 11 x 747-300, 4 x 747-400, 3 x 747SP, 8 x 777-200ER, 4 x Boeing (McDonnell Douglas) MD-11F, 16 x MD-90-30, 1 x Bombardier (Canadair) CL-604 Challenger, 2 x Cessna 550 Citation II, 2 x Dassault Falcon 900, 1 x de Havilland Canada DHC-6 Twin Otter 300, 4 x Gulfstream II, 2 x Gulfstream III, 6 x Gulfstream IV, 17 x Lockheed L-1011-200 TriStar, 1 x McDonnell Douglas DC-8-63 (leased).
On order: 1 x Boeing 747-400, 9 x 777-200ER, 12 x Boeing (McDonnell Douglas) MD-90-30
Colour Scheme: A new corporate identity was unveiled on 16 July 1996. The fuselage features selected shades of dune beige and white, separated by a gold pencil line, while the royal blue tail is dominated by a striking representation of the date palm and crossed swords in gold, and enclosed by a golden crescent above a turquoise sea. 'SAUDI ARABIAN' titles are inscribed in English, followed by 'Al Saudia' in Arabic characters, which literally means 'The airline of Saudi Arabia'. The royal blue and turquoise colours were inspired by the coral reefs and deep waters of the Red Sea and, together with the new rendering of the airline's symbol, were chosen to convey stature and dignity.
Illustrated: Boeing 747-400

SCANDINAVIAN AIRLINES SYSTEM
— SAS (SK/SAS)

Founded: 31 July 1946 **Bases:** Stockholm-Arlanda Airport, Sweden, Oslo Gardermoen, Norway and Copenhagen Airport, Denmark

Services: Tri-national airline operating an extensive domestic and intro-Scandinavian route system, together with scheduled services between Scandinavia and Europe, the Middle East and Far East, and the United States, reaching a total of 105 cities in 34 countries. This is further extended through its membership of the *Star Alliance*, which also

Scandinavian Airlines

includes Lufthansa, Air Canada, Thai International, United and Varig, and partial ownership of regional feeder airlines within Scandinavia and British Midland in the UK. SAS Commuter flies turboprop aircraft within Scandinavia and northern Europe, operating as EuroLink, NorLink and SweLink from bases at Copenhagen, Stockholm and Tromso.

Subsidiaries and Associates: SAS Commuter (100%), Air Botnia (100%), Greenlandair (37.5%), Wideroe's (29%), Cimber Air (26%), Skyways (25%), Spanair (49%), Airlines of Britain (40%), Air Baltic (34%)

Fleet: 5 x Boeing 737-600, 1 x 767-200ER, 15 x 767-300ER, 37 x Boeing (McDonnell Douglas) MD-81, 14 x MD-82, 2 x MD-83, 18 x MD-87, 8 x MD-90-30, 16 x Fokker F28-4000 Fellowship, 4 x McDonnell Douglas DC-9-21, 24 x DC-9-41. **On order:** 47 x Boeing 737-600

SAS Commuter: 22 x Fokker 50, 6 x Saab 2000. **On order:** 15 x Bombardier DHC-8Q-400

Colour Scheme: SAS introduced a new corporate identity on 24 September 1998. Developed by Sthlm Lab and the London-based design firm of Dieffenbach Elkins Davies Baron, the keywords of the new identity are seasons, colours and purity, simplicity and professionalism, the modern and innovative, informal elegance and hospitality — concepts that should reflect the personality of the airline. The exterior of the aircraft is intended to radiate safety and technical competence. The traditional 'SAS' logo is highlighted in white on a blue tail, setting off the winter white and autumn colours of the fuselage on which the word 'Airlines' is sketched near the front. Most of the engine cowlings are painted in colours of an orange-red sunset, with the words 'Scandinavian' reversed out in white. Stylised flags of the three owner nations are applied on the lower front fuselage, together with the logo, and at the rear above the windows. The Star Alliance symbol is displayed behind the cockpit windows.

Illustrated: Boeing 737-600

SINGAPORE AIRLINES (SQ/SIA)

Founded/First: Service: 28 January 1972/1 October 1972
Base: Changi International Airport, Singapore
Services: National flag-carrier operating daily flights to 40 countries linking 76 cities in Europe, Africa, the Middle East, Asia, South West Pacific and North America. Long-haul flight destinations serve Amsterdam, Athens, Berlin, Brussels, Copenhagen, Frankfurt, Istanbul, London Heathrow, Madrid, Manchester, Paris, Rome, Vienna and Zürich in Europe; Adelaide, Auckland, Brisbane, Cairns, Christchurch, Darwin, Melbourne, Perth and Sydney in the South West Pacific; Cairo, Cape Town, Dubai, Jeddah, Johannesburg and Mauritius in Africa and the Middle East; and Chicago, Los Angeles, New York (JFK and Newark), San Francisco and Vancouver in North America. Three freighter-only services are operated to Bangalore, Dublin and Sharjah. Subsidiary SilkAir serves 21 regional destinations in eight countries.
Subsidiaries and Associates: SilkAir (100%)
Fleet: 1 x Airbus A310-200, 17 x A310-300, 13 x A340-300, 4 x Boeing 747-300, 37 x 747-400, 8 x 747-400F, 10 x 777-200.
On order: 4 x Airbus A340-300, 5 x A340-500 (plus 5 options),
8 x Boeing 747-400 (plus 10 options), 2 x 747-400F, 20 x 777-200 (plus 31 options)
SilkAir: 2 x Airbus A320-200, 5 x Boeing 737-300, 2 x Fokker 70. **On order for subsidiary:** 4 x Airbus A319, 2 x A320-200
Colour Scheme: The all-white fuselage displays dramatic foreshortened cheatlines in midnight blue and yellow, below blue 'SINGAPORE AIRLINES' titles. The lower yellow 'laser' line widens to the rear and is repeated on the vertical stabiliser in order to communicate precision. A large stylised yellow bird hovers on the otherwise blue tail fin and is repeated in miniature on each engine. The corporate identity was created by Walter Landor Associates in 1972 and given a new logotype and other modifications in 1987.
Illustrated: Airbus A310-300

SINGAPORE AIRLINES LIMITED

SOUTH AFRICAN AIRWAYS
— SAA (SA/SAA)

Founded: 1 February 1934
Base: Johannesburg International Airport, Johannesburg, Republic of South Africa
Services: National flag-carrier operating intercontinental long-haul flights to Europe, Asia,
Australia and North and South America, together with regional flights within Africa.
Destinations are Abidjan, Accra, Amsterdam, Bangkok, Buenos Aires, Blantyre, Bulawayo,
Dakar, Dar-es-Salaam, Dubai, Frankfurt, Harare, Hong Kong, Kinshasa, Lilongwe, London
Heathrow, Luanda, Lusaka, Maputo, Mauritius, Miami, Mumbai (Bombay), Nairobi, New York,
Osaka, Paris, Perth, Sal Island, São Paulo, Sydney, Tel Aviv, Victoria Falls,
Windhoek and Zürich. Domestic trunk routes link Bloemfontein, Durban,
East London, George, Johannesburg, Cape Town and Port Elizabeth.
Subsidiaries and Associates: SA Express (76%), Alliance Air (40%), SA
Airlink (franchise)
Fleet: 4 x Airbus A300B2-3C, 3 x A300B4-200, 1 x A300C4-200,
7 x A320-200, 11 x Boeing 737-200 Advanced, 2 x 737-200F,
5 x 747-200B(SCD), 1 x 747-200F, 2 x 747-300, 5 x 747-400, 4 x 747SP, 3 x 767-200ER
On order: 1 x Boeing 747-400
Historic Flight: 1 x CASA 352L (Junkers Ju52/3M), 2 x Douglas DC-3, 2 x DC-4, 2 x Harvard
SA Express: 6 x Bombardier CRJ-200ER, 6 x DHC-8-300E
Colour Scheme: SAA's livery is based on the national flag of gold, black and green, displayed
prominently on the tail fin, where it is set between a blue field at the base and red at the top
of the tail. The red encloses a golden sun disk, symbolising the new beginning. The fuselage is
all-white with simple 'SOUTH AFRICAN' titles applied in blue on the forward fuselage. A small
flag appears under the rear windows.
Illustrated: Boeing 747-400

SUDAN AIRWAYS (SD/SUD)

Founded/First Service: 1946/April 1947
Base: Civil Airport, Khartoum, Sudan
Services: Domestic and international scheduled and charter passenger services to Abu Dhabi, Addis Ababa, Athens, Cairo, Damascus, Doha, Dubai, Frankfurt, Jeddah, Johannesburg, Kano, London Heathrow, Muscat, Nairobi, N'Djamena, Riyadh, Rome, Sana'a and Sharjah. Domestic routes provide vital links between the capital and such towns and cities as Atbara, Dongola, Elfasher, Elgeneina, Elobeid, Elrosieres, Juba, Kassala, Malakal, Merawe, Nyala and Port Sudan.
Fleet: 1 x Airbus A300-600, 1 x A310-300, 1 x Beechcraft C90 King Air, 1 x Super King Air 2000, 3 x Boeing 707-320C, 2 x 737-200C Advanced, 1 x de Havilland Canada DHC-6 Twin Otter 300, 2 x Fokker 50
Colour Scheme: The Sudan Airways scheme has changed little since first introduced in July 1974, but is still noticeable for its imaginatively styled elongated 'S' (for Sudan), which sweeps along in triple bands of Nile blue and sand yellow, starting below the cockpit windows, but soon stepping up to above the window line. The design then opens out at the tail fin, where the predominant colour is yellow, broken only by 'SUDAN' titles near the leading-edge. A small Sudanese flag is carried behind the forward cabin door.
Illustrated: Airbus A310-300

119

SWISSAIR (SR/SWR)

Founded/First Service:
16 March 1931
Base: Zürich Kloten Airport, Zürich,
Switzerland
Services: National flag-carrier with a
worldwide scheduled passenger and cargo network serving more than 150 destinations in 80
countries on all continents. Extensive European services reach all capitals together with many
other major cities from Helsinki in the North, to Malta in the South. Connections between
Switzerland and the Americas serve Atlanta, Boston, Buenos Aires, Chicago, Cincinnati, Los
Angeles, Montreal, Mexico City, New York, Philadelphia, Rio de Janeiro, Santiago de Chile,
São Paulo, San Francisco and Washington, some served jointly with other carriers. Swissair
heads the *Qualiflyer* alliance, which also includes Air Littoral, Austrian Airlines, AOM French
Airlines, Sabena, Turkish Airlines, TAP Air Portugal, as well as its regional subsidiary Crossair.
Subsidiaries and Associates: Crossair (70.9%), LTU (49.9%), Sabena (49.5%), Air Europe Italy,
Air Littoral (44%), Volare, Austrian Airlines (10%), Delta Air Lines (4.5%), Singapore Airlines
(0.6%)
Fleet: 6 x Airbus A310-300, 8 x A319-100, 19 x A320-200, 9 x A321-100, 1 x A330-200,
5 x Boeing 747-300, 15 x Boeing (McDonnell Douglas) MD-11
On order: 1 x Airbus A320-200, 1 x A321-100, 14 x A330-200, 9 x A340-600, 4 x Boeing
(McDonnell Douglas) MD-11
Colour Scheme: Like all Swiss airlines, Swissair is instantly recognisable by the white holy cross
of the national flag, which goes right back to the Battle of Laupen in 1339 and is emblazoned
on a bright red tail. Bold red 'swissair' titles are carried on the forward white upper fuselage,
which extends down to wing level before giving way to a purple underside.
Illustrated: Airbus A330-200

SYRIANAIR (RB/SYR)

Founded: October 1961 as Syrian Arab Airlines, but trading as Syrianair
Base: Damascus International Airport, Damascus, Syrian Arab Republic
Services: National flag-carrier providing international scheduled passenger and cargo services to destinations within Syria and to points in Europe, North Africa, and the Middle East and Far East. Cities on the network include Abu Dhabi, Algiers, Amsterdam, Athens, Bahrain, Beirut, Berlin, Bucharest, Budapest, Cairo, Damascus, Delhi, Dhahran, Doha, Dubai, Frankfurt, Istanbul, Jeddah, Karachi, Khartoum, Kuwait, Larnaca, London Heathrow, Madrid, Moscow, Mumbai (Bombay), Munich, Muscat, Paris Orly, Prague, Riyadh, Rome, Sana'a, Sharjah, Sofia, Stockholm, Tehran and Tunis. Domestic services link Damascus with Aleppo, Deirezzor and Latakia.
Fleet: 1 x Airbus A320-200, 1 x Antonov An-24, 5 x An-26, 6 x Boeing 727-200 Advanced, 2 x 747SP, 2 x Dassault Falcon 20F, 4 x Ilyushin Il-76M, 6 x Tupolev Tu-134B-3, 3 x Tu-154M, 5 x Yakovlev Yak-40 (some aircraft operated by the Syrian Air Force in Syrianair colours)
On order: 5 x Airbus A320-200
Colour Scheme: The Syrian national flag-carrier has replaced its long-standing corporate identity with a bright new modern look. A bright Mediterranean blue tail fin incorporates the company's symbol, a stylised mythical bird flying across the sun, and is repeated on the engine cowlings. The only other adornment on a fresh white fuselage are 'SYRIAN' titles in the same blue below the forward windows, with red Arabic titles above.

Illustrated: Airbus A320-200

TAP AIR PORTUGAL (TP/TAP)

Founded/First Service: 14 March 1945/September 1946
Base: Lisbon Airport, Lisbon, Portugal
Services: National flag-carrier with an extensive European network and flights to Africa and North and South America, and the Far East. European destinations are Amsterdam, Athens, Barcelona, Berlin, Bologna, Brussels, Copenhagen, Frankfurt, Geneva, Hamburg, Hannover, London Heathrow, Luxembourg, Lyon, Madrid, Milan, Munich, Nice, Oslo, Paris, Rome, Stockholm, Vienna and Zürich. A domestic route system includes Faro, Funchal, Horta, Lisbon, Oporto, Ponta Delgada, Porto Santo and Terceira.
Fleet: 5 x Airbus A310-300, 6 x A319-100, 6 x A320-200, 4 x A340-300, 4 x Boeing 737-200 Advanced, 8 x 737-300
On order: 10 x Airbus A319-100, 2 x A321-200
Colour Scheme: The red and white 'TAP' logo (from Transportes Aéreos Portugueses) flies up the white tail, followed by a red 'contrail' trimmed above in green, which forms the cheat line to the nose of the aircraft. The 't' in the 'tap' lettering appears in outline, while the others are in solid red. The top half of the aircraft above wing level is painted white, with the natural metal finish below. Black 'AIR PORTUGAL' titles on the cabin roof are preceded by the Portuguese flag. Green and red are the national colours.
Illustrated: Airbus A340-300

TAROM ROMANIAN AIR TRANSPORT (RO/ROT)

Founded: 1946 as TARS, present title adopted in 1954
Base: Otopeni International and Baneasa airports, Bucharest, Romania
Services: National airline operating scheduled passenger and cargo services within Romania, and to points in Europe, Africa, the Middle East and Far East, and the United States. Cities on the route system include Abu Dhabi, Amman, Amsterdam, Athens, Bangkok, Barcelona, Belgrade, Beirut, Berlin, Brussels, Budapest, Cairo, Copenhagen, Delhi, Dubai, Düsseldorf, Frankfurt, Istanbul, Kiev, Kishinev, Kuwait, London Heathrow, Larnaca, Madrid, Moscow, New York JFK, Paphos, Paris CDG, Prague, Rome, Sofia, Tel Aviv, Vienna, Warsaw and Zürich. Also flies a comprehensive domestic network serving 12 major towns and cities.
Fleet: 2 x Airbus A310-300, 6 x Antonov An-24RV, 2 x ATR42-300, 6 x ATR42-500, 5 x Boeing 737-300, 2 x 707-320C, 6 x British Aerospace (BAC) 111-500, 5 x Rombac 1-11-560, 7 x Tupolev Tu-154B.
On order: 1 x Airbus A310-300
Colour Scheme: The livery design displays large 'TAROM' titles in dark blue below the window line, and forward of the all-white fuselage, underscored by a speed line extending to the rear. The blue tail incorporates the airline's long-standing bird symbol inside double rings, both in white.
Illustrated: Airbus A310-300. *Terry Shone*

THAI AIRWAYS INTERNATIONAL
(TG/THA)

Founded: 24 August 1959
Base: Don Muang International Airport, Bangkok, Thailand
Services: National airline with an extensive regional network and services to Europe, North America and Australia and New Zealand serving 73 cities in 35 countries. Intercontinental destinations include Amsterdam, Athens, Auckland, Brisbane, Copenhagen, Dubai, Frankfurt, London Heathrow, Los Angeles, Madrid, Melbourne, Munich, Muscat, Paris, Perth, Rome, Stockholm, Sydney and Zürich. The airline is part of the Lufthansa and United Airlines-led *Star Alliance*, which also includes Air Canada, SAS and Varig. Major routes in a comprehensive 22-point domestic system link Bangkok, Chiang Mai, Hat Yai, Nakon Ratchasima, Phuket and Surat Thani.
Fleet: 2 x ATR42-300, 2 x ATR72-200, 1 x Airbus A300B4-100, 6 x A300-600, 15 x A300-600R, x A310-200, 11 x A330-300, 11 x Boeing 737-400, 1 x 747-200F, 2 x 747-300, 14 x 747-400, 8 x 777-200, 2 x 777-300, 4 x Boeing (McDonnell Douglas) MD-11, 3 x McDonnell Douglas DC-10-30ER.
On order: 1 x Airbus A330-300, 1 x Boeing 747-400, 4 x 777-300
Colour Scheme: Thai's visual appearance was created by leading design consultants Walter Landor Associates and introduced in 1975. Its rich and vibrant colours vividly reflect culture and country. Opulent gold, pink and purple tones recall the gold of the temples, the brilliant hues of the orchids and the intensity of Thailand's famous shimmering silks, all incorporated in an enormous stylised orchid symbol on the tail dominating the all-white fuselage. A smaller version speeds ahead of a gold, purple, gold cheat line, which runs the whole length of the aircraft. The abbreviated purple 'THAI' logo is displayed near the front passenger door.
Illustrated: Boeing 747-400

TNT INTERNATIONAL AVIATION SERVICES (NTR)

Founded/First Service: 1946 (in Australia)/5 May 1987 (in Europe)

Services: Scheduled express overnight cargo services operated for parent company TNT International by a number of European airlines, including its own airlines Pan Air of Spain and Mistral Air of Italy, plus Air Foyle in the UK, and Denmark's Sterling European. Among scheduled destinations are Athens, Barcelona, Basle, Belfast, Bergamo, Billund, Birmingham, Brussels, Budapest, Cologne, Copenhagen, Geneva, Gothenburg, Helsinki, Istanbul, Lisbon, Liverpool, London Stansted, Lyon, Madrid, Malmö, Nuremberg, Oslo, Paris CDG, Prague, Rome, Stockholm, Valencia, Vienna and Zaragoza. European services are supported out of Manila by Pacific East Asia Cargo (PEAC). TNT also provides contracted and ad hoc charters, concentrating on the thoroughbred racehorse industry, as well as newspapers, racing cars and the automotive industry.

Fleet: 1 x Airbus A300B4-200F, 9 x Boeing 727-200F, 9 x British Aerospace 146-200QT, 9 x 146-300Q

Colour Scheme: TNT replaced the red 'TNT' initials in a compartmented black box on the tail fin with a new corporate image in 1998. The forward fuselage is now completely surrounded in bright orange, with the rear section in white with a bold black cheat line. The company's new motif of three linked circles with the TNT letters, both in orange with black shadows, features aft of the wings and on the tail fin.

Illustrated: Airbus A300B4-200F

TRANSAERO AIRLINES (4J/TSO)

Founded/First Service: 28 December 1990
Base: Moscow Sheremetyevo Airport, Moscow, Russian Federation
Services: Major Russian airline providing services within Russia, the Commonwealth of Independent States (CIS), Europe and the United States. Destinations include Almaty, Ashkhabad, Baku, Berlin Schönefeld, Cairo, Chicago, Eilat, Ekaterinburg, Frankfurt, Hong Kong, Irkutsk, Kiev, Kishinev, Krasnoyarsk, London Gatwick, Los Angeles, Minsk, Nizhnevartovsk, Novosibirsk, Norlisk, Odessa, Orlando, Omsk, Paris CDG, Riga, Sochi, St Petersburg, Tashkent, Tel Aviv, Vladivostok and Yuzho-Sakhalinsk. New York will be added in 1999. The Riga-London Gatwick service is operated as an extension of the Moscow-Riga route by associate Riair. Feeder and executive services within Russia are flown by Transaero Express.
Subsidiaries and Associates: Transaero Express (100%), Riair (30%)
Fleet: 5 x Boeing 737-200 Advanced, 2 x 737-700, 5 x 757-200, 1 x 767-300ER, 1 x Ilyushin IL-86, 2 x McDonnell Douglas DC-10-30
On order: 6 x Ilyushin IL-96M
Colour Scheme: The simple livery of Russia's second international airline comprises a red gradated arrow in the national colours of red and blue, flying up the white tail fin. Blue 'TRANSAERO' titles are painted on the forward cabin roof. The upper fuselage of the aircraft is Arctic white, going over into a grey lower half just below the window line.
Illustrated: Ilyushin IL-86. *Terry Shone*

TRANSAVIA AIRLINES (HV/TRA)

Founded/First Service: 1965/17 November 1966
Base: Amsterdam Schiphol Airport, Amsterdam, The Netherlands
Services: Subsidiary of KLM Royal Dutch Airlines providing a scheduled business connection between Amsterdam and London Gatwick, in addition to scheduled 'leisure' flights to the Mediterranean basin resort areas and to Madeira and the Canary Islands. Destinations are Alicante, Barcelona, Casablanca, Djerba, Faro, Funchal, Heraklion, Izmir, Las Palmas de Gran Canaria, Lisbon, Malaga, Malta, Nice, Palma de Mallorca, Rhodes and Tenerife. Charter flights are also operated to over 60 points in Europe, accounting for a large part of the Dutch charter market, and for French, German and Italian tour operators. Spare capacity, especially in the winter period, is leased out to other airlines.
Fleet: 14 x Boeing 737-300, 3 x 737-800, 4 x 757-200
On order: 5 x Boeing 737-800 (plus 12 further options)
Colour Scheme: Developed in co-operation with more than 200 employees, the Transavia scheme emphasises such concepts as strength, dynamism, enthusiasm and personal attention. A bold green flash strikes from nose to tail on a brilliant white fuselage, broadening out towards the rear. An elegant and flowing stylised 'T' in blue and green is featured on the tail fin. Blue 'Transavia' titles are placed above the forward cabin windows and repeated on the outboard face of the white engine cowlings. The present corporate identity was introduced on 20 February 1995.
Illustrated: Boeing 737-800. *Capital Photos*

TRANS WORLD AIRLINES
— TWA (TW/TWA)

Founded/First Service: 13 July 1925/17 April 1926
Base: St Louis International Airport, St Louis, Missouri, United States
Services: US major operating an extensive domestic trunk network, together with flights to Canada, Mexico, the Caribbean, and across the Atlantic to Europe, North Africa and the Middle East, serving more than 100 destinations. Another 40 domestic feeder routes are operated by associate Trans States Airlines under the *Trans World Express* banner. International destinations include Athens, Barcelona, Cairo, Cancun, Copenhagen, Frankfurt, Istanbul, Ixtapa/Zihuatanejo, Lisbon, London, Madrid, Mexico City, Milan, Montego Bay, Paris, Puero Vallarta, Riyadh, Rome, San Juan, Santo Domingo, Stockholm and Tel Aviv.
Fleet: 18 x Boeing 727-200, 11 x 727-200 Advanced, 15 x 757-200, 9 x 767-200ER, 2 x 767-300ER, 37 x Boeing (McDonnell Douglas) MD-82, 26 x MD-83, 7 x McDonnell Douglas DC-9-15, 18 x DC-9-31, 14 x DC-9-32, 1 x DC-9-33F, 3 x DC-9-34, 3 x DC-9-41, 12 x DC-9-51.
On order: 50 x Airbus A318, 25 x A320-200, 10 x A330-300, 4 x Boeing 757-200, 26 x Boeing (McDonnell Douglas) MD-83
Colour Scheme: TWA's present livery was introduced with the delivery of the Boeing 757 in July 1996. A broad warm red and thinner gold cheat line sit atop the midnight blue of the underside of the aircraft, and provide separation from the snow-white top. The three colours extend up the rear of the tail fin, supporting the traditional red 'TWA' initials. Elegantly understated 'TRANS WORLD' titles, taking up most of the fuselage, end in a stylised golden globe.
Illustrated: Boeing 757-200

TWA®

TUNISAIR (TU/TAR)

Founded/First Service: 1948
Base: Carthage International Airport, Tunis, Tunisia
Services: Tunisian flag-carrier providing international scheduled services linking Tunis to destinations in Europe, the Middle East, and North and West Africa. Points served include Abu Dhabi, Algiers, Amman, Amsterdam, Athens, Barcelona, Berlin, Bordeaux, Bratislava, Brussels, Budapest, Cairo, Casablanca, Copenhagen, Dakar, Damascus, Düsseldorf, Frankfurt, Geneva, Hamburg, Istanbul, Jeddah, Khartoum, Lille, Lisbon, London Heathrow, Luxembourg, Lyon, Madrid, Malta, Marseille, Milan, Moscow, Munich, Nice, Nouakchott, Palermo, Paris Orly, Prague, Rome, Strasbourg, Toulouse, Warsaw and Zürich. Domestic services are also flown, some in association with Tuninter, linking Tunis, Monastir, Djerba, Sfax and Tozeur.
Subsidiaries and Associates: Tuninter (40%)
Fleet: 1 x Airbus A300B4-200, 2 x A319-100, 8 x A320-200, 8 x Boeing 727-200 Advanced, 3 x 737-200 Advanced, 1 x 737-200C Advanced, 4 x 737-500
On order: 1 x Airbus A319-100, 4 x A320-200, 4 x Boeing 737-600
Colour Scheme: The present livery was adopted with the introduction into service of the Airbus A320 in October 1990. It is centred on an all-white fuselage highlighted by a red flying gazelle on the tail fin. The impression of speed has been created with red pinstripes trailing down the fin and around the rear fuselage. Red 'TUNISAIR' titles in English and Arabic are displayed on the cabin roof, with the Tunisian flag near the rear.
Illustrated: Airbus A320-200

TURKISH AIRLINES — THY (TK/THY)

Founded/First Service: 20 May 1933 as Devlet Hava Yollari (DHY), changed to Turk Hava Yollari (THY), of which the present title is the English equivalent, in February 1956

Base: Atatürk International Airport, Yesilköy, Istanbul, Turkey

Services: National airline providing international passenger and cargo services to 64 cities, with a strong emphasis on Europe, which link Istanbul and Ankara with 37 destinations. Points served in Central Asia, North Africa, the Middle and Far East, and the United States include Abu Dhabi, Amman, Ashkhabad, Bahrain, Baku, Bangkok, Beijing, Beirut, Bishkek, Cairo, Chicago, Damascus, Dubai, Jakarta, Jeddah, Johannesburg, Karachi, Kuwait, New York, Osaka, Riyadh, Seoul, Singapore, Tashkent, Tehran, Tokyo and Tunis. The domestic network includes all the major cities and tourist resorts of Istanbul, Ankara, Izmir, Dalaman, Antalya, Adana, Gaziantep, Diyarbakir, Van, Erzurum and Trabzon, as well as many more secondary destinations.

Fleet: 7 x Airbus A310-200, 7 x A310-300, 5 x A340-300, 3 x Boeing 727-200 Advanced, 30 x 737-400, 2 x 737-500, 2 x British Aerospace (Avro) RJ70, 10 x RJ100

On order: 2 x Airbus A340-300, 23 x Boeing 737-800

Colour Scheme: The national colours of red and white predominate on the current scheme, with a red tail fin riding the all-white fuselage. Set into a white circle on the fin is the airline's bird symbol in red. Blue 'TURKISH' titles are followed by a small Turkish flag, which includes the crescent moon and star on a red field, associated with the Ottoman Empire. All aircraft carry names of Turkish towns and cities.

Illustrated: Airbus A310-300

TURKISH AIRLINES

UKRAINE INTERNATIONAL AIRLINES (PS/AUI)

Founded/First Service: October 1992/November 1992 as Air Ukraine International
Base: Kiev Borispol Airport, Kiev, Ukraine
Services: International flag-carrier providing scheduled passenger services from the capital Kiev to several European cities, including Amsterdam, Barcelona, Berlin, Brussels, Frankfurt, London Gatwick, Madrid, Manchester, Munich, Paris Charles de Gaulle, Rome, Vienna and Zürich. Some UK frequencies are operated via Lvov, and there is also a Kiev-Donetsk domestic service. Long-haul connections are available at Vienna and Zürich through associated carriers Austrian Airlines and Swissair, which have an 18.3% stake in the airline.
Fleet: 2 x Boeing 737-200 Advanced, 2 x 737-300.
On order: 1 x Boeing 737-300
Colour Scheme: Ukraine International uses the national colours of blue and yellow to good effect. The blue of the tail fin is carried down in line with the leading-edge and wrapped around the fuselage behind a broad band of yellow. A highly stylised bird symbol flies on a yellow disk set into the blue tail. 'Ukraine International Airlines' titles, preceded by the national flag, are carried on the forward fuselage above the window line, while the full title appears in the local language below the windows.
Illustrated: Boeing 737-300

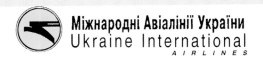

UNITED AIRLINES (UA/UAL)

Founded/First Service: 1 July 1931, but ancestor airlines go back to 1926
Base: Chicago O'Hare International Airport, Chicago, Illinois, United States
Services: World's second-largest airline providing scheduled passenger and cargo services from hubs at Chicago, Denver, Los Angeles, San Francisco and Washington Dulles to 99 US cities and 37 international airports, serving 28 countries and one US territory. Another 186 airports are served by its six United Express partners. The network extends throughout North America, and to Central and South America, Europe, and across the Pacific to Asia, Australia and New Zealand. A round-the-world service links Los Angeles, New York, London, Delhi and Hong Kong. United is part of the global *Star Alliance*, which also includes Lufthansa, Air Canada, SAS, Thai Airways International and Varig.
Subsidiaries and Associates: United Express: Air Wisconsin Airlines, Atlantic Coast Airlines, Great Lakes Aviation, Mountain West Express, SkyWest Airlines and Westair.
Fleet: 15 x Airbus A319, 50 x A320-200, 75 x Boeing 727-200 Advanced, 5 x 737-200, 24 x 737-200 Advanced, 101 x 737-300, 57 x 737-500, 6 x 747-100, 9 x 747-200B, 34 x 747-400, 96 x 757-200, 19 x 767-200, 27 x 767-300ER, 34 x 777-200, 22 x McDonnell Douglas DC-10-10, 4 x DC-10-30, 4 x DC-10-30F
On order: 33 x Airbus A319, 35 x A320-200, 17 x Boeing 747-400, 2 x 757-200, 10 x 767-300ER, 18 x 777
Colour Scheme: United's elegant business-like scheme features a combination of a silver-grey upper fuselage and striped tail fin, with alternative mid-blue and dark blue stripes. The blue and red corporate 'double U' outlined in white, is set into the top half of the fin. Triple pinstripes in orange, red and blue separate the upper fuselage from the deep midnight blue belly of the aircraft. White 'UNITED AIRLINES' titles are displayed at the front.
Illustrated: Boeing 777-200

UNITED PARCEL SERVICE (UPS)
(5X/UPS)

Founded/First Service: 1983
Base: Louisville, Kentucky, USA
Services: One of the world's biggest transportation companies providing cargo and express package delivery services to more than 200 countries and territories, offering next-day and two-day delivery service to anywhere in the world. In addition to its primary hub at Louisville, UPS operates regional hubs across the United States and Canada at Hartford, Miami, Ontario, Philadelphia, Rockford, Hamilton and Montreal, and international hubs at Cologne/Bonn in Germany, Hong Kong (China) and Taipei in Taiwan.
Fleet: 51 x Boeing 727-100F, 10 x 727-200F, 16 x 747-100F, 73 x 757-200PF, 22 x 767-300F, 23 x McDonnell Douglas DC-8-71F, 26 x DC-8-73F
On order: 30 x Airbus A300F4-600R, 2 x Boeing 757-200PF, 8 x 767-300F
Another 302 aircraft are chartered from and operated by other airlines
Colour Scheme: Using a dark chocolate brown as the predominant colour, the UPS scheme displays a traditional 'straight through' window line, which extends at the rear to fill the tail fin. The company shield, displaying 'UPS' lettering beneath a 'wrapped' parcel, appears in gold outline and forms the central feature of the tail. Bold brown 'United Parcel Service' lettering is carried on the forward fuselage.
Illustrated: Boeing 767-300F

US AIRWAYS (US/USA)

Founded/First Service: 5 March 1937/13 September 1937 as All-American Aviation, present title adopted 27 February 1997

Base: Pittsburgh International Airport, Pennsylvania, and Charlotte Douglas International, North Carolina, United States

Services: Fifth-largest US airline operating vast domestic network connecting 104 destinations throughout the United States, serving 38 states, the District of Columbia, Commonwealth of Puerto Rico and the US Virgin Islands, plus Montreal, Ottawa and Toronto in Canada, Bermuda, Curaçao, Grand Cayman, Kingston, Mexico and Nassau. Another 175 destinations are served by nine regional carriers operating under the US Airways Express banner in US Airways colours. US Airways Shuttle flies frequent services between New York LaGuardia, Boston and Washington DC, while low-fare subsidiary MetroJet serves the eastern seaboard and Florida. Transatlantic flights serve Amsterdam, Frankfurt, London (Gatwick), Madrid, Paris and Rome.

Subsidiaries and Associates: MetroJet (100%), US Airways Shuttle (100%), *US Airways Express:* Allegheny Airlines (100%), Piedmont Airlines (100%), PSA Airlines (100%), Air Midwest Airlines, CCAir, Chautauqua Airlines, CommutAir, Mesa Airlines and Trans States Airlines.

Fleet: 5 x Airbus A319, 64 x Boeing Boeing 737-200 Advanced, 85 x 737-300, 54 x 737-400, 34 x 757-200, 12 x 767-200ER, 19 x Boeing (McDonnell Douglas) MD-81, 12 x MD-82, 40 x Fokker 100, 48 x McDonnell Douglas DC-9-32.

On order: 104 x Airbus A319, 15 x A320-200

US Airways Shuttle: 8 x Boeing 727-200, 4 x 727-200 Advanced. *Allegheny Airlines:* 37 x Bombardier DHC-8-100. *Piedmont Airlines:* 40 x Bombardier DHC-8-100, 10 x DHC-8-200.

PSA Airlines: 25 x Fairchild Dornier 328-110

Colour Scheme: With the recent change of name, the airline changed its livery to reflect its experience as an international airline. Designed by New York-based Deskey Design Associates, the aircraft feature a near midnight blue upper fuselage, separated from the lower grey by narrow red and white cheat lines below the windows. The blue extends up to cover most of the tail fin, which is again topped by white and red, and displays a stylised *Stars and Stripes* in grey. This also appears ahead of the 'US AIRWAYS' titles along mid-fuselage. Associated regional carriers have the word 'Express' added.

Illustrated: Airbus A319

UZBEKISTAN AIRWAYS (HY/UZB)

Founded/First Service: 28 January 1992
Base: Yuzhnyy International Airport, Tashkent, Uzbekistan
Services: National airline providing flag services from Tashkent and Uzbekistan's second city Samarkand to Europe, the Middle and Far East, and the United States. Destinations include Almaty, Amsterdam, Ashkhabad, Athens, Bahrain, Baku, Bangkok, Beijing, Bishkek, Chelyabinsk, Delhi, Ekaterinburg, Frankfurt, Istanbul, Jeddah, Karachi, Kazan, Khabarovsk, Kiev, Krasnodar, Krasnoyarsk, Kuala Lumpur, London Heathrow, Maldives, Mineralnye Vody, Moscow, New York JFK, Novosibirsk, Omsk, Rostov, St Petersburg, Seoul, Sharjah, Simferopol, Tel Aviv, Tyumen and Ufa. Special aerial work services are provided by associate SAR.
Subsidiaries and Associates: Spetsialnye Aviatsionnye Raboty (SAR)
Fleet: 3 x Airbus A310-300, 2 x Antonov An-12B, 23 x An-24V/RV, 1 x Boeing 757-200, 2 x 767-300ER, 3 x British Aerospace (Avro) RJ85, 12 x Ilyushin IL-62M, 15 x IL-76TD, 10 x IL-86, 2 x IL-114, 8 x Tupolev Tu-154B-2, 3 x Tu-154M, 28 x Yakovlev Yak-40
SAR: 24 x Mil Mi-8, 116 x PZL Mielec (Antonov) An-2, 8 x PZL Swidnik (Mil) Mi-2
Colour Scheme: A sky blue fuselage roof and grass green belly, both outlined by a red pencil line and starting behind the cockpit, frame the white mid-part of the fuselage, which sports black 'UZBEKISTAN' titles. The fuselage paint scheme closely mirrors the national flag. The sky blue tail features the airline symbol of a stylised dove in green, flying across a gold sun disk encircled in red. The symbol is also displayed on the blue engine cowlings.
Illustrated: Airbus A310-300

VARIG
BRAZILIAN AIRLINES (RG/VRG)

Founded/First Service: 7 May 1927/3 February 1928
Base: Antonio Carlos Jobim International Airport, Rio de Janeiro, Brazil
Services: Brazil's major international airline, operating extensive
domestic and regional scheduled passenger and cargo services, as
well as intercontinental long-haul flights to destinations in Europe,
West Africa, southern Africa, the Far East, Mexico and the United
States, serving 35 cities in 23 countries. Transatlantic and
Transpacific destinations include Amsterdam, Bangkok, Barcelona,
Copenhagen, Frankfurt, Hong Kong, Johannesburg, Lisbon,
London Heathrow, Madrid, Oporto, Paris CDG, Rome, Milan, Nagoya, Tokyo and Zürich. The
domestic network, together with subsidiaries Rio-Sul and Nordeste, encompasses more than 40
major towns and cities throughout Brazil. Varig is a member of the global *Star Alliance*, which also
includes Lufthansa, United Airlines, Air Canada, SAS and Thai Airways International, giving it access
to many more points worldwide.
Subsidiaries and Associates: Rio-Sul Serviços Aéreos Regionais (96.79%), Nordeste Linhas Aéreas
Regionais
Fleet: 5 x Boeing 727-100F, 18 x 737-200 Advanced, 33 x 737-300, 3 x 747-300, 2 x 747-300 Combi,
6 x 767-200ER, 6 x 767-300ER, 9 x Boeing (McDonnell Douglas) MD-11,
6 x McDonnell Douglas DC-10-30, 2 x DC-10-30CF.
On order: 25 x Boeing 737-700/800, 6 x 767-300ER, 8 x 777-200
Rio-Sul: 14 x Boeing 737-500, 13 x Embraer EMB-120ER Brasilia, 10 x ERJ-145, 7 x Fokker 50.
Nordeste: 2 x Boeing 737-500, 6 x Embraer EMB-120ER Brasilia, 2 x Fokker 50
Colour Scheme: Varig's corporate identity, introduced in late 1996, is said to represent success,
dynamism and the Brazilian spirit. It is distinguished by a navy tail fin and engine cowlings, with the
underbelly accented with a lighter blue on an otherwise white fuselage. The long-standing compass
insignia has been restyled in two hues of yellow, suggesting the warmth of the sun and the lustre of
gold. Traditional 'VARIG' titles in matching blue are followed by 'BRASIL' in gold script. The Brazilian
flag is painted on the rear fuselage.
Illustrated: Boeing (McDonnell Douglas) MD-11

VIRGIN ATLANTIC AIRWAYS (VS/VIR)

Founded/First Service: June 1982/22 June 1984
Bases: London Heathrow and Gatwick airports, United Kingdom
Services: The UK's second-largest long-haul carrier operating scheduled value-for-money passenger services from London Heathrow, London Gatwick and Manchester. Services from Heathrow are flown to Hong Kong, Johannesburg, Miami, Los Angeles, New York JFK and Newark, San Francisco, Tokyo and Washington, while Boston, New York Newark and Orlando are served from Gatwick, with the last-named also from Manchester. Athens is scheduled from both London airports. A major alliance partnership with Continental Airlines gives Virgin access to Continental's large US network from New York. A low-cost Virgin Sun charter operation has been set up at Manchester, and the Virgin group also controls low-fare scheduled airline Virgin Express, based at Brussels.
Subsidiaries and Associates: Virgin Express (90%), Virgin Sun (100%)
Fleet: 1 x Airbus A320-200, 10 x A340-300, 1 x Boeing 747-100, 5 x 747-200B, 7 x 747-400
On order: 8 x Airbus A340-600
Colour Scheme: A slight adjustment to the livery was announced on 3 July 1997, following British Airways' decision to drop the Union flag from its aircraft. Since then, Virgin's 'Scarlet Lady' emblem has been holding the fluttering Union flag aloft, as she flies on the front of the fuselage. The all-white aircraft are dominated by the orange-red tail fin, sporting the well-known 'Virgin' signature in white. Other distinguishing features, also highly visible from afar, are the orange-red engine cowlings and winglets. The initial letter 'V' from the signature appears on the latter.
Illustrated: Boeing 747-400

YEMENIA YEMEN AIRWAYS (IY/IYE)

Founded/First Service: 1954 as Yemen Airlines, adopted present name 1 July 1978
Base: Sana'a International Airport, Sana'a, Yemen
Services: National airline operating scheduled international flag services for passengers and freight from Sana'a and Aden to other points in the Middle East, and to Africa, Europe and the Indian subcontinent. Destinations include Abu Dhabi, Addis Ababa, Amman, Amsterdam, Bahrain, Cairo, Damascus, Dhahran, Djibouti, Doha, Dubai, Frankfurt, Istanbul, Jeddah, Karachi, Khartoum, Larnaca, London Gatwick, Madrid, Moscow, Mumbai (Bombay), Nairobi, Paris Orly, Riyadh, Rome and Sharjah. A domestic network serves 10 destinations, including the main towns of Aden, Hodeidah, Sana'a and Taiz.
Fleet: 2 x Airbus A310-300, 5 x Boeing 727-200 Advanced, 2 x 737-200 Advanced, 1 x 737-200C Advanced, 2 x de Havilland Canada DHC-6 Twin Otter 300, 4 x DHC7-100, 2 x Lockheed L-382C Hercules. A number of government-owned Antonov An-12, An-24, An-26 aircraft and one Ilyushin IL-76TD are operated in Yemenia markings.
Colour Scheme: The aircraft livery alludes to the national flag and employs the bright red and royal blue on the tail fin, dissected by the company motif of a wing section behind the Islamic red crescent on an oval white field. 'Yemenia' titles in blue, in both English and Arabic, follow the national flag on the forward all-white fuselage. The tail design is repeated on the engine cowlings.
Illustrated: Airbus A310-300

AIRCRAFT NATIONALITY AND REGISTRATION MARKS

An organised systematic approach to the registration of civil aircraft was first proposed as early as 1912, but due to the intervention of World War 1, it was not instituted until the Paris Air Convention in 1919. It was then recommended that all aircraft should have five letters with the first denoting the nationality. All letters were to be painted in black on white as large as possible on both sides of the fuselage as well as on the top surface and underside of the wings. In addition, the nationality letter was to be painted on each side of the tailplane. Privately owned aircraft had to have the last four letters underlined.

As a result of the rapid development of civil aviation, almost all countries owned aircraft by 1929 and the regulations were revised accordingly. Gradually, however, many of these rules were forgotten with registrations becoming smaller and the nationality letter on the tail disappearing altogether. The present standards adopted by the International Civil Aviation Organisation (ICAO) on 8 February 1949 call for registrations to be applied on the upper half of the vertical tail surface, but this is rarely adhered to. They should also be clean, clearly visible and identifiable.

With the exception of the national prefix, which has been adopted by all the member nations, the individual aircraft registration is issued subject to the country's own internal regulations for civil aircraft. These are usually in the form of three or four letters (depending on whether a one- or two-letter national prefix is allocated) either in alphabetical or numerical sequence. Some nations have their own subdivisions, which serve to group individual aircraft types and thus assist in recognition (eg SE-**H** for helicopters). In many countries, major airlines are given a special sequence which makes them instantly recognisable: such examples are ZS-**SA**… for South African Airways, HS-**T**… for Thai International, N670**UA** for United Airlines, etc.

List of aircraft nationality registrations notified to the International Civil Aviation Organisation

Listed in alphabetical country order

Afghanistan	YA
Albania	ZA
Algeria	7T
American Samoa	N
Andorra	C3
Angola	D2
Anguilla	VP-LA
Antigua and Barbuda	V2
Argentina	LV/LQ
Armenia	EK
Aruba	P4
Australia	VH
Austria	OE
Azerbaijan	4K
Bahamas	C6
Bahrain	A9C
Bangladesh	S2
Barbados	8P
Belarus	EW
Belau (Palau)	-
Belgium	OO
Belize	V3
Benin	TY
Bermuda	VP-B
Bhutan	A5
Bolivia	CP
Bosnia-Herzegovina	T9
Botswana	A2
Brazil	PP/PT
British Virgin Islands	VP-LV
Brunei	V8
Bulgaria	LZ

139

Country	Code	Country	Code
Burkina Faso	XT	Guinea-Bissau	J5
Burundi	9U	Guyana	8R
Cambodia	XU	Haiti	HH
Cameroon	TJ	Honduras	HR
Canada	C-F/C-G	Hungary	HA
Cape Verde Republic	D4	Iceland	TF
Cayman Islands	VP-C	India	VT
Central African Republic	TL	Indonesia	PK
Chad	TT	Iran	EP
Chile	CC	Iraq	YI
China, People's Republic	B	Ireland	EI
China (Hong Kong)	B-H	Israel	4X
Colombia	HK	Italy	I
Comoro Republic	D6	Ivory Coast	TU
Congo (Brazzaville)	TN	Jamaica	6Y
Congo,		Japan	JA
Democratic Republic	9Q/9T	Jordan	JY
Costa Rica	TI	Kazakhstan	UN
Croatia	9A	Kenya	5Y
Cuba	CU	Kiribati	T3
Cyprus	5B	Korea, People's Republic	P
Czech Republic	OK	Korea, Republic	HL
Denmark	OY	Kuwait	9K
Djibouti	J2	Kyrgyzstan	EX
Dominica	J7	Laos	RPDL
Dominican Republic	HI	Latvia	YL
Ecuador	HC	Lebanon	OD
Egypt	SU	Lesotho	7P
El Salvador	YS	Liberia	EL
Equatorial Guinea	3C	Libya	5A
Eritrea	E3	Lithuania	LY
Estonia	ES	Luxembourg	LX
Ethiopia	ET	Macau	CS-M
Falkland Islands	VP-F	Macedonia	Z3
Fiji	DQ	Madagascar	5R
Finland	OH	Malawi	7Q
France	F	Malaysia	9M
French Overseas		Maldives	8Q
Departments	F-O	Mali	TZ
Gabon	TR	Malta	9H
Gambia	C5	Marshall Islands	V7
Georgia	4L	Mauritania	5T
Germany	D	Mauritius	3B
Ghana	9G	Mexico	XA/B/C
Gibraltar	VP-G	Micronesia	V6
Greece	SX	Moldova	ER
Grenada	J3	Monaco	3A
Guatemala	TG	Mongolia	JU
Guinea	3X	Montserrat	VP-LM

Morocco	CN	Liechtenstein	HB
Mozambique	C9	Syria	YK
Myanmar	XY	Taiwan (Republic of China)	B
Namibia	V5	Tajikistan	EY
Nauru	C2	Tanzania	5H
Nepal	9N	Thailand	HS
Netherlands	PH	Togo	5V
Netherlands Antilles	PJ	Tonga	A3
New Zealand	ZK	Trinidad and Tobago	9Y
Nicaragua	YN	Tunisia	TS
Niger	5U	Turkey	TC
Nigeria	5N	Turkmenistan	EZ
Norway	LN	Turks and Caicos Islands	VQ-T
Oman	A4O	Tuvalu	T2
Pakistan	AP	Uganda	5X
Palestine	OD	Ukraine	UR
Panama	HP	United Arab Emirates	A6
Papua New Guinea	P2	United Kingdom	G
Paraguay	ZP	United States of America	N
Peru	OB	Uruguay	CX
Philippines	RP	Uzbekistan	UK
Poland	SP	Vanuatu	YJ
Portugal	CS	Vatican	HV
Qatar	A7	Venezuela	YV
Romania	YR	Vietnam	VN
Russian Federation	RA	Western Samoa	5W
Rwanda	9XR	Yemen	7O
San Marino	T7	Yugoslavia, Federal Republic	YU
Sao Tomé e Principe	S9	Zambia	9J
Saudi Arabia	HZ	Zimbabwe	Z
Senegal	6V		
Seychelles	S7	*Listed in registration prefix order*	
Sierra Leone	9L		
Singapore	9V	AP	Pakistan
Slovak Republic	OM	A2	Botswana
Slovenia	S5	A3	Tonga
Solomon Islands	H4	A4O	Oman
Somalia	6O	A5	Bhutan
South Africa	ZS	A6	United Arab Emirates
Spain	EC	A7	Qatar
Sri Lanka	4R	A9C	Bahrain
St Kitts and Nevis	V4	B	China, People's Republic
St Lucia	J6	B	Taiwan (Republic of China)
St Vincent and Grenadines	J8	B-H	China (Hong Kong)
Sudan	ST	C-F/C-G	Canada
Surinam	PZ	CC	Chile
Swaziland	3D	CN	Morocco
Sweden	SE	CP	Bolivia
Switzerland and		CS	Portugal

CS-M	Macau	J2	Djibouti
CU	Cuba	J3	Grenada
CX	Uruguay	J5	Guinea-Bissau
C2	Nauru	J6	St Lucia
C3	Andorra	J7	Dominica
C5	Gambia	J8	St Vincent and Grenadines
C6	Bahamas	LN	Norway
C9	Mozambique	LV/LQ	Argentina
D	Germany	LX	Luxembourg
DQ	Fiji	LY	Lithuania
D2	Angola	LZ	Bulgaria
D4	Cape Verde Republic	N	United States of America
D6	Comoro Republic	N	American Samoa
EC	Spain	OB	Peru
EI	Ireland	OD	Lebanon
EK	Armenia	OD	Palestine
EL	Liberia	OE	Austria
EP	Iran	OH	Finland
ER	Moldova	OK	Czech Republic
ES	Estonia	OM	Slovak Republic
ET	Ethiopia	OO	Belgium
EW	Belarus	OY	Denmark
EX	Kyrgyzstan	P	Korea, People's Republic
EY	Tajikistan	PH	Netherlands
EZ	Turkmenistan	PJ	Netherlands Antilles
E3	Eritrea	PK	Indonesia
F	France	PP/PT	Brazil
F-O	French Overseas Departments and Territories	PZ	Suriname
		P2	Papua New Guinea
		P4	Aruba
G	United Kingdom	RA	Russian Federation
HA	Hungary	RDPL	Laos
HB	Switzerland and Liechtenstein	RP	Philippines
		SE	Sweden
HC	Ecuador	SP	Poland
HH	Haiti	ST	Sudan
HI	Dominican Republic	SU	Egypt
HK	Colombia	SX	Greece
HL	Korea, Republic	S2	Bangladesh
HP	Panama	S5	Slovenia
HR	Honduras	S7	Seychelles
HS	Thailand	S9	Sao Tomé e Principe
HV	Vatican	TC	Turkey
HZ	Saudi Arabia	TF	Iceland
H4	Solomon Islands	TG	Guatemala
I	Italy	TI	Costa Rica
JA	Japan	TJ	Cameroon
JU	Mongolia	TL	Central African Republic
JY	Jordan	TN	Congo (Brazzaville)

Prefix	Country	Prefix	Country
TR	Gabon	ZP	Paraguay
TS	Tunisia	ZS	South Africa
TT	Chad	Z3	Macedonia
TU	Ivory Coast	3A	Monaco
TY	Benin	3B	Mauritius
TZ	Mali	3C	Equatorial Guinea
T2	Tuvalu	3D	Swaziland
T3	Kiribati	3X	Guinea
T7	San Marino	4K	Azerbaijan
T9	Bosnia-Herzegovina	4L	Georgia
UK	Uzbekistan	4R	Sri Lanka
UN	Kazakhstan	4X	Israel
UR	Ukraine	5A	Libya
VH	Australia	5B	Cyprus
VN	Vietnam	5H	Tanzania
VP-B	Bermuda	5N	Nigeria
VP-C	Cayman Islands	5R	Madagascar
VP-F	Falkland Islands	5T	Mauritania
VP-G	Gibraltar	5U	Niger
VP-LA	Anguilla	5V	Togo
VP-LM	Montserrat	5W	Western Samoa
VP-LV	British Virgin Islands	5X	Uganda
VQ-T	Turks and Caicos Islands	5Y	Kenya
VT	India	6O	Somalia
V2	Antigua and Barbuda	6V	Senegal
V3	Belize	6Y	Jamaica
V4	St Kitts and Nevis	7O	Yemen
V5	Namibia	7P	Lesotho
V6	Micronesia	7Q	Malawi
V7	Marshall Islands	7T	Algeria
V8	Brunei	8P	Barbados
XA/B/C	Mexico	8Q	Maldives
XT	Burkina Faso	8R	Guyana
XU	Cambodia	9A	Croatia
XY	Myanmar	9G	Ghana
YA	Afghanistan	9H	Malta
YI	Iraq	9J	Zambia
YJ	Vanuatu	9K	Kuwait
YK	Syria	9L	Sierra Leone
YL	Latvia	9M	Malaysia
YN	Nicaragua	9N	Nepal
YR	Romania	9Q/T	Congo, Democratic Republic
YS	El Salvador	9U	Burundi
YU	Yugoslavia, Federal Republic	9V	Singapore
YV	Venezuela	9XR	Rwanda
Z	Zimbabwe	9Y	Trinidad and Tobago
ZA	Albania	-	Belau (Palau)
ZK	New Zealand